Educational Credential Analysis

A Comprehensive Resource for World Educational Credentials

Dr. Raghu Korrapati, Ph.D., D.Sc., D.Litt.

DIAMOND BOOKS

www.diamondbook.in

Publisher : **Diamond Pocket Books (P) Ltd.**
X-30, Okhla Industrial Area, Phase-II
New Delhi-110020

Phone : 011-40712200
E-mail : sales@dpb.in
Website : www.diamondbook.in
Editorials : Saif Nadeem

Educational Credential Analysis
By – Dr. Raghu Korrapati

Contact the Author:
Website: http://www.edu-evals.com **E-mail:** eduevals@gmail.com
Phone: +1- (803) 422 6397 EDT **Fax:** +1-(866) 292 1949

Dedicated to

Avyaan

Parents & Grand parents

Preface

It is often said by those who are entrenched in the field of educational credential evaluation that it is a "lonely job" – many evaluators work in institutions or regulatory bodies without others actually understanding their work. This is because despite credential evaluation being intricately and inevitably a part of the engines of education globally, there exist no set standards by which evaluators can function in collaboration with each other. Indeed, credential evaluation, credit transfer and grade translation are among the most widely debated and highly sensitive issues in international education.

There is tremendous ambiguity surrounding this field. It is compounded by the fact that grading systems differ widely in theory and practice from one country to another, and the fair interpretation of foreign grades into national ones is a major concern, both for students returning after a study period abroad and for university staff required to assess the credentials of foreign applicants. The academic world, especially students, struggle to determine what their education amounts to in another country. I have worked in the field of education for close to three decades now in various roles, and I have repeatedly pondered on the plight of Indian students who wish to study in the USA as well as those who apply for jobs there. These students and young professionals are bright, have tremendous potential to be great employees to American employers or even pioneers in their respective fields. The only thing they need is – access to the right institutions abroad that can harness this potential. Furthermore, this access is severely hampered by the ambiguity and lack of standards which I have highlighted above.

With this in mind, I have used my own knowledge, gathered over several years in the educational field, as well as a lot of meticulous research, to come up with a work that aims to make things much easier especially for students. I have attempted to do this by providing detailed overviews of the Indian and the American education. The credential evaluation component also exists outside of the academic community: at state licensing boards and other types of governmental agencies, at professional associations, and at private foreign educational credential evaluation services which assist institutions and agencies that do not have in-house expertise. This book is also aimed to facilitate the smoother functioning of these institutions.

Below is a reference list of people in specific roles who should "hire" this book to help them do the following "jobs":

- Admission Counselors/Admission Officers - Admission Counselors should "hire" this book to evaluate a student's foreign degree credentials, understand foreign education system, and the grading system in different countries among others.
- Prospective Students - Prospective Students should "hire" this book to learn about the "education culture" in different countries, mode of entries in different countries, degree requirements, credential evaluation, grading system, application steps among others.
- Parents/Guardians - Parents/Guardians should "hire" this book to learn about the "education culture" in different countries, mode of entries in different countries, degree requirements, credential evaluation, grading system, application steps among others.
- Employers - Employers should "hire" this book to learn

criteria about foreign degree evaluations for international hires.

- Licensors - They should "hire" this book to learn criteria about foreign degree evaluations for international credentials.
- Immigration Attorneys - Immigration Attorneys should "hire" this book to learn about legalization of credentials, and foreign degree evaluations on behalf of employers hiring specialized knowledge professionals.

I hope you enjoy reading this book as much as I enjoyed writing it!

Contents

Chapter One
Background and Concept

Concepts of Foreign Studies

A Foreign or International study is an act of moving beyond national borders to further or begin one's education, mostly to attain a degree or certification of some kind. It has been a popular and on-going move for many years that even nowadays people tend to value it more than degrees earned within the country. Many students have desires to study in a foreign institution, obviously for different purposes though. This not only adds to international development and relations but also creates a more elaborate platform whereby ideas and knowledge can be shared and acted upon.

Students who choose to study in a different nation or country apart from their home country and migrate to the country for study purpose are called international students. [1]According to statistics in the year 2016, students who study in foreign countries were above five million, which is between two to three percent of the total tertiary student populace. Comparing that with the data from the year 2000, we have an incremental of over two million students who study abroad. [2]Regardless of the huge measure of private and public assets spent on foreign

1 "What defines an international student". University World News. 20 September 2009.

2 "Democracy and Foreign Education" Antonio Spilimbergo. Vol. 99, No. 1 (Mar., 2009), pp. 528-543

studies, there is no efficient proof that foreign-educated people encourage majority rule government in their nations of origin. According to research, it was found that people who had foreign education advance majority rules system in their nation of origin, but only if they obtained it in a developed country.

The meaning of "foreign student" and "international student" differs in every nation in agreement to their very own educational framework. Students who are studying on a temporary or immigration visa in the United States for educational purpose at the post-secondary stage are called International students. Some categories of individuals are excluded from this particular definitions, like; natives, citizens, immigrants, and Green Card holders.

In Canada, they describe an international student as someone who is an impermanent inhabitant with an approval to undergo any form of education or study in the country; the immigration agency gives this approval. This kind of grant is accompanied by the permitted timeframe the individual must spend in the country to study. International students need not bother with a study grant for courses which runs for half-year or less in the event that they will complete the course within time of stay approved upon entry, which is typically a half-year. All international students are requested to have a permit of study, and there could be various kinds of grants and authorization attached too.

In Australia, an individual from another nation with a study permit to get any form of education in Australia with any institution within the country through a student visa is referred to as an international student. Some categories of students are exempted from this requirement of getting a student visa before getting to study in the country, like students from New Zealand.

In Japan, a student that is not from Japan and is aspiring to get educated at any institution within the country is called an international or foreign student. This also refers to someone who resides in the country with a student visa.

Although many countries accept foreign students in their institution, only a few of them are highly recognized for their massive intake of foreign students every year (Table 1.1). Under this study, only the top countries with colossal foreign education activities and also with credential evaluation would be explored.

Table 1.1 Foreign Students Intake by Top Countries.

[3]Rank	Destination country	Foreign students (2018)	Foreign students (2017)	% change	Top sending countries
1	United States	1,094,792	1,078,822	+1.48%	China, India, South Korea
2	United Kingdom	506,480	501,045	+1.08%	China, United States, Germany
3	China	489,200	442,773	+10.49%	South Korea, Thailand, Pakistan
4	Australia	371,885	327,606	+13.52%	China, India, Nepal
5	Canada	370,710	312,100	+18.78%	China, India, South Korea
6	France	343,386	323,933	+6.01%	Morocco, Algeria, China
7	Russia	313,089	296,178	+5.71%	Kazakhstan, China, Uzbekistan
8	Germany	265,484	251,542	+5.54%	China, India, Russia
9	Japan	188,384	171,122	+10.09%	China, Vietnam, Nepal
10	Spain	109,522	94,962	+15.33%	Italy, France, the United States

3 "Current Infographics". Institute of International Education. Dr. Constantinos K. Coursaris.

Functionality of Foreign Studies

There are many functions of foreign studies, most people refer to them as "benefits" but seeing there are complications and challenges, it would be safer to term them as functions. The list below shows the different purposes of foreign studies (Fig 1).

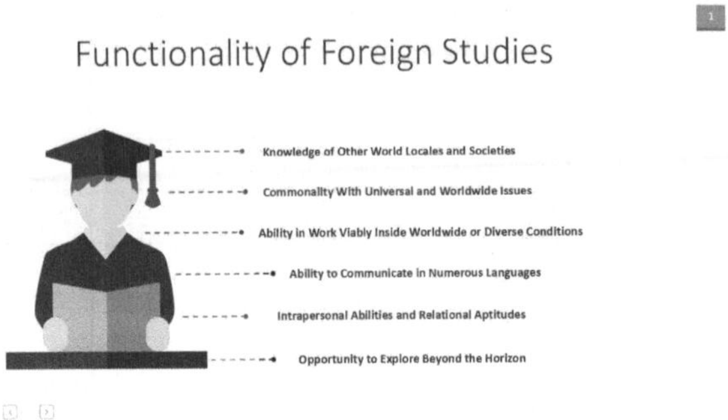

Figure 1 Functionality of Foreign Studies.

1. [4]**Knowledge of Other World Locales And Societies:** Being educated in a foreign nature gives you a Global Mindset. In terms of relations, Culture influences individuals to see each other better. Furthermore, on the off chance that they see each other better in their spirit, it is simpler to defeat the financial and political hindrances. In any case, the first thing to learn is to comprehend that all races are alike in a lot of ways, with similar issues and inquiries. The scheme about studying abroad is increasingly about the time which is spent in learning another nation's way of life and having a remarkable experience.
2. [5]**Commonality With Universal And Worldwide Issues:** By living and studying in a foreign country, you'll figure out

4 "Five reasons why studying abroad is a good idea" indiatoday.com

5 "10 Benefits to Studying Abroad" internationalstudent.com

how to battle with the reality of being far from home. From enrolling with a nearby specialist to making dinner with strange ingredients, or notwithstanding, calling a locksmith in an unknown dialect on the off chance that you've bolted yourself out, you'll continually be compelled to step up to the plate and take care of issues. After this; applying your collected, even-minded, and critical thinking aptitudes in the realm of business will be a thing of ease. Foreign study alludes to a dynamic idea that includes an adventure or development of individuals, brains, or thoughts crosswise over many frontiers; it is globally encouraged.

3. [6]**Ability In Work Viably Inside Worldwide Or Diverse Conditions:** When you study abroad, you open new doors of assistance to build up your skills. Training is one of the critical factors that you should deal with while choosing a nation to study. There are numerous variables an individual must remember while selecting a country or a school. Each nation and its separate schools have an alternate arrangement of standards, traditions and instruction designs that shape their understudies. Regardless of which campus you find yourself on, you should represent one of the hundreds of nationalities around you. Making acquaintances globally makes an individual smarter, as regular opportunities are encountered to challenge beliefs and enjoy exposure to an amazing variety of customs and cultures. It also stands as a big résumé-uplift, you might decide or plan to work for an international company or move into a sector such as non-profit, government, international business or finance. Employers value the skills and characteristics cultivated by studying in a foreign country, including adaptability,

6 "7 Career Benefits of Studying Abroad" topuniversities.com

independence, and resilience; in addition, the preparation it provides for working in a multi-cultural domain.

Moreover, the course of study trains an individual to understand an extensive parameter of business contexts and needs universally, as well as giving the chance to spend some time somewhere else in the world, gathering knowledge. It gives you a vast range of career opportunity and personal development.

4. **Ability To Communicate In Numerous Languages:** If you desire to have your education in a foreign nation, you should be set up to gain proficiency with an unknown dialect. Regardless of whether it includes learning another dialect or getting conversant in one, concentrating in an alternate country includes social and lingual assorted variety. If an individual has an intense desire to learn a new language, there is no better way to learn that studying in that country where the language is originated.
5. **Intrapersonal Abilities And Relational Aptitudes:** Going to an alternate nation for training includes meeting new individuals and fabricating an international system of contacts. Imagine a different environment which supports your certainty and causes you to exceed expectations in numerous parts of life and your aptitudes.
6. **Opportunity To Explore Beyond The Horizon:** Foreign study has a ton of advantages as one gets the opportunity to make a trip and becomes acquainted with various societies. Additionally, you get the chance to encounter better places, and you become more acquainted with various individuals with various convictions that widen your reasoning. Being educated abroad is an undertaking of a lifetime as you investigate the world in your school life.

Accredited Agencies

[7]**Credentials** are generally termed educational and academic qualifications, for example, diplomas or degree that have accomplished or partially accomplished. It can likewise be referred to as occupational qualifications, like professional certificates or work experience.

[8]**Credential Evaluation** can be defined or termed as a process by which professional or academic degrees earned or received in a country are juxtaposed with ones gotten from another country. Universities, colleges and businesses around the globe use credential assessments to comprehend foreign studies and to pass judgment on candidates for confirmation or employment. So, how does an institution validate or acknowledge the certifications or credentials of a foreign student? Credentials evaluators come in to play here. They play an important role in this educational transformation for students wanting to study abroad. Credential evaluators process on a well-figured moral standard and serve individuals who have finished part or the majority of their education outside their host nation and who are looking for further education overseas, or even proficient licensure or work.

Migrants can utilize Credential assessments to pick up acknowledgment for study finished outside the nation they are moving to and in the process join the workforce or labor market as capable immigrants. Credential evaluation is mostly utilized by foreign students to introduce or present their achieved coursework from an institution in a country to institutions anywhere in the world for admission consideration.

---

7 "What are Credentials" Ontario Council of Agencies Serving Immigrants (OCASI)

8 "What is a Credential Evaluation?" World Education Services

The objective of accreditation is to guarantee that higher education institutions meet satisfactory dimensions of value. Accreditation's quality affirmation purpose is one of the three principal components of oversight administering the Higher Education Act's federal student aid programs. An institution must be certified by a federally recognized accreditor or in some cases, endorsed by a recognized state endorsement agency, be approved by the state in which the establishment is found, and get an endorsement from the Department of education through a program interest consensus before the country recognizes it and worldwide as an accredited institution.

Credential Evaluation in The United States

[9]The United States is one of the biggest countries where educational activities take place on the planet, and there is a colossal inpouring of international students. The assorted variety of candidates and their separate education frameworks requires a shared opinion for evaluating educational credentials.

Credential evaluators in the US run three types of evaluations (Fig 2):

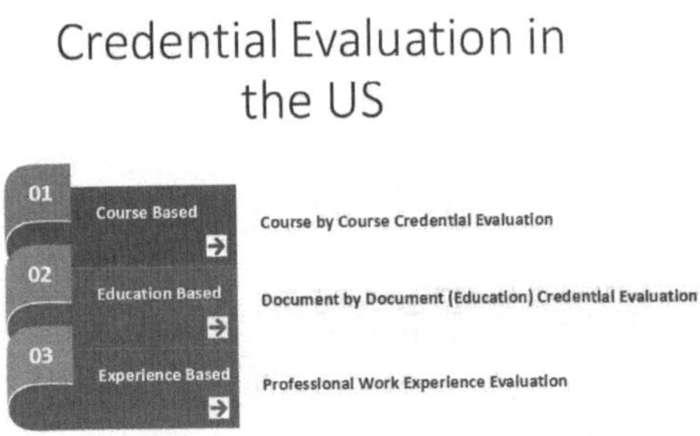

9 "Project Atlas". Institute of International Education.

Figure 2 Credential Evaluation in the US.

Course by Course Credential Evaluation

The course by course qualification assessment report recognizes and gives a description for every certificate or diploma and gives an equivalency for distinct documents. It demonstrates a portrayal of the time span of education, courses, credit hours, evaluations, degrees, and comprehensive performance as far as the educational framework in the United States or your host nation.

Educational Credential Evaluation (Document By Document)

The document by document qualification evaluation report depicts and records the educational institution(s) visited, and the credential(s) earned in a foreign nation and states their U.S. proportionality. For example; Bachelor, Master, Doctorate, and so forth. This kind of qualification assessment is most regular for use in securing jobs, migration matters and university or college admission purpose when transfer credit comes unexpectedly.

Professional Work Experience Evaluation_

The Professional work experience credential assessment is made available for immigrants applying for H-1B visas in the United States. This credential evaluation report assesses a person's professional work history and academic qualifications so as to set up equivalence for a Bachelor's degree. This sort of credential evaluation can't be utilized for educational or licensure reasons.

10 "Have Your Education Assessed - Skilled Immigrants (Express Entry)". Citizenship and Immigration Canada. Government of Canada

Credential Evaluation in Canada

[10]In Canada, it is generally known as Educational Credential Assessment (ECA) otherwise called Credential Evaluation. It can be utilized for permits, education, and immigration. This type of assessment is important for settlers looking for express entry into the country through the Federal Skilled Worker Program (FSWP) and different Citizenship and Immigration Canada (CIC) programs. Nevertheless, there is a prerequisite that the individual must have finished at least something that corresponds with a Secondary School Diploma in Canada. The CIC assigned seven credential assessment agencies to give appraisals to those moving to Canada since April 2013; therefore, the government is not concerned with the evaluation of foreign certifications. Most Canadian permitting boards or professional authorizing bodies require an academic credential assessment from universally educated professionals. The assessments are evaluated internally or done by Alliance members.

Credential Evaluation in Europe

[11]In Europe, it is generally called the **Lisbon Recognition Convention**. It involves the convention on the recognition of the credentials involving Higher education in the European province. The convention implies that degree holders should have access to adequate assessments of their qualifications and degrees should be acknowledged among the native country except if there are validated substantial differences between the awarded degrees in that nation and the degree being evaluated.

11 "The Lisbon Recognition Convention". Enic-Naric. European Network of Information Centres in the European Region and National Academic Recognition Information Centres in the European Union.T

12. "Qualifications Recognition". Department of Education and Training. Australian Government.

Credential Evaluation In Australia

[12]In Australia, the whole system is quite different from other countries; they do not use the platform to assess credential. Skill assessment is done by the authority to evaluate and validate credentials for the purpose of skilled migration. And it must be done according to the occupation the individual nominates. An evaluating authority is a body that checks if an individual meets the standards they set. The principles include university or trade educations for a particular occupation. The evaluation needs to be validated and prove that the individual has the relevant skills to support the application.

Credential Evaluation in the Middle East

[13]In the Middle East, there was a convention held in the Arab states in the year 1978, it was based on the acknowledgment of Studies, Degrees, and Diploma in Higher Education. The purpose of the convention was to adopt evaluation standards and terminology relatively so as to develop a framework which guarantees the equivalence and comparability of coursework, credits, and diplomas. Moreover, it was to encourage student movement beyond borders. Eighteen states made an agreement to the convention. Unlike many other countries, this system has proved to be peculiar.

Following are the list of foreign Accredited Evaluation Agencies:

- Foreign Credential Evaluator (FCE).
- Education Records Evaluation Service (ERES).
- Foreign Academic Credential Service (FACS).
- NASBA International Evaluation Services (NIES).

13 "Convention on the Recognition of Studies, Diplomas and Degrees in Higher Education in the Arab States 1978". United Nations Educational, Scientific and Cultural Organization. United Nations.

- Foreign Educational Document Service (FEDS).
- Academic and Credential Records Evaluation and Verification Service (ACREVS).
- SpanTran Evaluation Services (SES).
- Academic Records Evaluation Center (AREC).
- Foreign Credentials Service of America (FCSA).
- Josef Silny & Associates (JS&A).
- American Education Research Corporation (AERC).
- International Credential Assessment of Canada (ICAS).
- Academic and Professional International Evaluation (APIE).
- International Education Research Foundation (IERF).
- Foundation for International Services (FIS).
- Education Evaluators International (EEI).
- Center for Applied Research, Evaluation, and Education (IESCAREE).
- Academic Credentials Evaluation Institute (ACEI).
- Comparative Education Service (CES).
- Center for Educational Documentation (CED).
- International Credential Evaluation Service (ICES).
- International Qualifications Assessment Service (IQAS).
- World Education Services (WES).
- Academic Evaluation Services (AES).
- Global Education Group (GEG).

The evaluating agencies are not limited to this list; there are also others who might not be so popular as these agencies. Moreover, more agencies are being established subsequently.

Procedures of Application

There are distinct procedures of application for different countries; some are technical while some are not. The following are the basic procedures on Foreign Credential Evaluation (Fig 3):

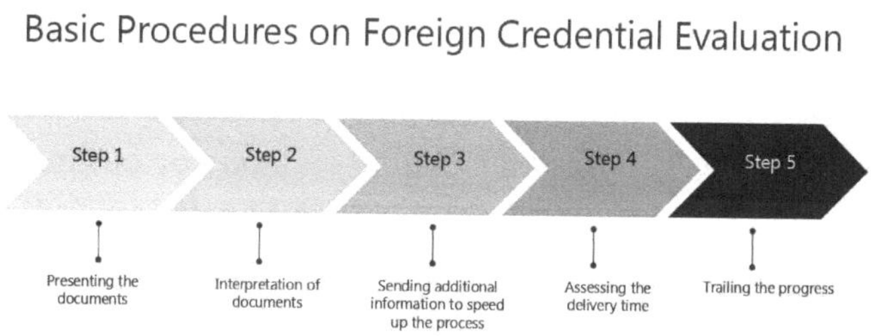

Figure 3 Basic Procedures on Foreign Credential Evaluation.

[14]**1. Presenting the Documents:** Several international credential assessment bodies demand the applicant to submit the authorized and certified transcript. The authorized transcript is the copy submitted directly from your former institution to the credential evaluation agency for evaluating purpose, be it official or original copy. The certified transcript is the copy provided by the same institution that is mailed in a closed envelope to you personally.

Many a time, this prerequisite is set by the state board. For instance, California state board requests that the evaluators issue report just if the applicant provides the original copy. If present applicant's name is not the same as the name on the transcript, there would be a need for supporting report (document) to prove the reason of the change in name, e.g., a marriage certificate.

14 "Foreign Credential Evaluation for CPA" Stephanie Ng.

2. **Interpretation of Documents:** On the off chance that the transcript you are submitting in a language different from English, a thorough translation would be needed. You can investigate if necessary, for any internal interpretation or translation administration at the assessment agency office. You can also ask the assessment agency you are using; they could have a favored translation service they use for interpretations of documents.
3. **Sending additional information to speed up the Process:** You can also submit your course syllabus or outline to the agency to assist them so that they would have the full details of your credentials.
4. **Assessing the delivery Time:** The delivery period for every international credential evaluation body listed above should begin counting when every demanded material is submitted. For urgent service, it is measured in business days. For instance, a 2-day urgent service takes two business days.
5. **Trailing the Progress:** Few assessment agencies own online tracking systems which help to keep applicants updated by accessing the site, while some have email notification service. A couple of them have no updates, and you need to call them to keep track.

Credentials' Rating and Assessment

Below are some of the internationally known credentials;

[15]Academic Credentials:

- High-school Certificate
- College Certificate
- Bachelor's Degree (B.Sc.)
- Master's Degree (M.Sc.)
- Ph.D. or Doctorate
- Professional degree (teaching, law, medicine, etc.)

A lot of evaluating bodies assess foreign educational qualification to juxtapose them with qualifications that can be attained from the native country. It may be required for work or when applying to an institute, university or college. Research and find out the perfect place to get your qualifications assessed for employment or academic purpose.

Professional Certificates:

- Professional licenses
- Memberships in professional associations

Occupational Certificates:

- Trade certificates
- Apprenticeships
- Work experience

Many evaluation agencies could review the listed classes of qualifications, but not all. You should find out what these agencies can do for you.

15 "What are Credentials" Ontario Council of Agencies Serving Immigrants (OCASI)

Chapter Two
Academic Equivalency Evaluation

Mode of Entries in Different Countries

EVery country has a unique mode of entry into their various institutions, although some are similar; there are still diversities of the way foreign admission is handled. Since there are 195 countries in the world, it leaves the area of study too wide so only the various test and exams known to be taken by top-rated countries who are known to be academically active and where a lot of international education activities take place would be discussed.

The mode of entry for a foreign student is not too technical. All countries with higher education have different frameworks and are open to all candidates from everywhere throughout the world. Concerning every admission issue, every institution has a dependency on how they run foreign student admittance; therefore, a little bit of research has to be done by the applicant. The generally known and accepted mode of entry into any higher institution in a country is through the writing of some tests and the evaluation of results from the host country. There five commonly known tests that are taken before being considered for admission in the US (Fig 4), they are:

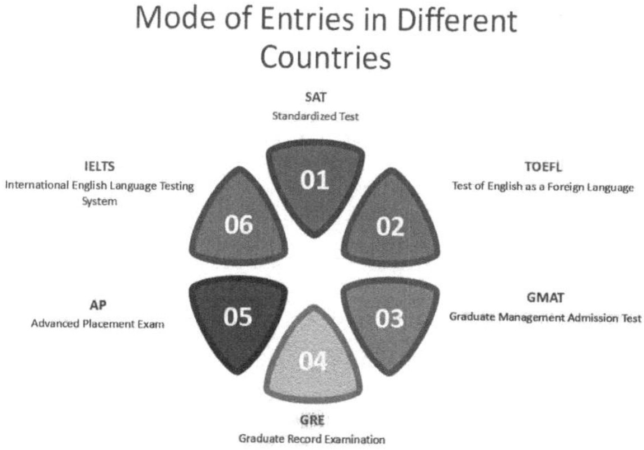

Figure 4 Mode of Entries in Different Countries.

[16]**Standardized Test (SAT):** It is an undergraduate test or exam that is required before being considered for admission into most of the colleges and universities in the many institutions. SAT involves mathematics, critical reading, and writing. SAT grades assist universities in translating a candidate's comprehensive academic performance in connection to the national candidate platform. Examples of Countries that accept SAT are; the United States, Canada, Japan, Australia, the Netherlands, Turkey, South Korea, Lebanon, Finland, the United Kingdom, Singapore, etc.

[17]Test of English as a Foreign Language (TOEFL): It is also a standardized test but it only a test to determine the English Language skill of the applicant, especially if the applicant is from a country where English is not a native language. It is a necessity for almost every student who desires to study in any English-speaking institution. It is known to be accepted in over ten thousand universities and many other institutions in the world Examples of Countries who accept TOEFL are; the United

16 "A look at exams required to study in the US" The Times of India
17 "The TOEFL® Test" ETS

States, Canada, the United Kingdom, New Zealand, Australia, etc. All institutions in Europe and Asia are recognized to accept TOEFL.

[18]**The Graduate Management Admission Test (GMAT):** It is a computer-based test for writing, verbal, quantitative, analytical writing and reading abilities in English. It is majorly used to gain admission into business schools. Over two thousand graduate business schools are known to categorize the GMAT as one of their requirements for any of their programs. Examples of Countries that accept GMAT are Finland, Denmark, the United States, India, Philippines, France, United Arab Emirates, Egypt, the United Kingdom, Australia, Turkey, Israel, Italy, etc.

[19]**Graduate Record Exam (GRE):** It is required for admission considerations in most of the non-business institutions in various countries. Students from everywhere across the universe who want to pursue a Master's degree, Doctoral degree or J.D. degree go for GRE test. It is accepted in numerous graduated schools across the world, in the Asian countries, the United States, Canada, the United Kingdom, France, etc.

[20]**Advanced Placement Exam (AP):** This consists of courses and tests done in preparation cross over to the university. Only secondary school students take this exam to get them ready for the university level. Over one hundred countries accept AP exam, e.g., the United States, Canada, Singapore, the United Kingdom, Australia, etc.

International English Language Testing System (IELTS): This is a universal commonly known English language test. It is a standardized test for international students who do not have English language as their native dialect.

---

18 "Learn About the GMAT Exam." Graduate Management Admission Council (GMAC).
19 "The GRE® General Test" ETS
20 "AP International" Education Professionals

Anyone who desires to study in a foreign country should consider taking this test. The grade is valid for two years. Examples of the Countries who accept IELTS are; Canada, Australia, the United Kingdom, New Zealand, etc.

The list of assessment tests above is the generally known tests accepted by many institutions, but they are not limited to them.

[21]Varieties of Degree in Various Countries

It is acknowledged that there are varieties of degrees in the world, so many qualifications that could be attained and they vary according to stages of other qualification attainments (Fig 5).

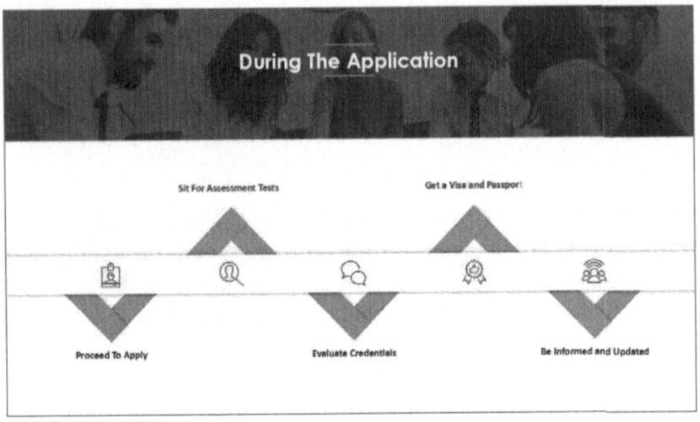

Figure 5 Varieties of Degrees.

Associate Degrees

Associate degrees regularly run for two years, and they are intended to furnish students with a fundamental handle on the subjects studied. Their principal point is to breed students for passage level positions in different fields, for example, nursing, education, designing, etc. A few individuals utilize this degree as the beginning stage of their professions while some people use it as a venturing stone towards the level of a higher degree, for example, a 4-year college education, called bachelor's degree in an academic term.

There are various distinctive sorts of degrees obtainable, they are:

Associate of Applied Science Degree: It is also commonly known as **A.A.S.** It is perfect for those students who are sure

21 "Levels of College Degrees You Should Know" Excite Education

about further education into a bachelor's degree. Sometimes, an associate degree is termed by the particular career path, for example, An Associate in Information Technology, Associate in Business, etc.

Associate of Science Degree (A.S): It is structured to be used to transfer to a bachelor's degree also.

Occupational certificate: It is fundamentally an associate program targeted at making students' prompt deployments when they are done with the study.

The conventional educational prerequisites for an associate degree are a secondary school certificate or corresponding credential. It is a degree that can be obtained online as well.

National Diploma (OND): This is a typical odinary academic qualification that is offered by most academic colleges in the country. The Diploma is utilized in numerous ways, many of the National Diplomas are rated at the third level on the National Qualifications System; however, some are at the fourth or fifth level which is termed as a higher level education. HND is ranked at level 5 on the framework for Higher Education Qualifications in England, Wales, and Northern Ireland. Certain professional National Diplomas are ranked at the sixth level; however, only independent bodies awarded this type of diploma, acknowledging professional study in a particular field.

[22]**Higher National Diploma (HND):** This is a form of higher education qualification in many countries like Finland (not termed official), Nigeria, Argentina, Ghana, Malta, India, and some other countries that have a bond with the British. This credential can be utilized to get admission into universities at an advanced dimension. It is also considered as a correspondent to the third year of a 4-year university degree course or the second

22 "Higher National Certificates and Higher National Diplomas" Directgov.

year of a 3-year university degree course, and in some cases, it is considered equal to a university degree. It is rated at the fifth level on the national qualification system in most countries like Ireland, England, and Wales.

Bachelor's Degrees

A Bachelor's Degree can be described as an undergraduate degree program that normally runs for four years. This can be taken in any form, any field of choice available in the academic platform, examples are: Statistics, Nursing, Arts, Computer Science, Pharmacy, Mass Communication, Computer Technology, Animal Science, Mathematics, Psychology, Business management, law, Physics, architecture, Music, Engineering, Zoology, Fisheries, Botany, Dentistry, Medicine, aeronautics, Films and TV, Human Science and so many more, there is a course of study for almost every ambition in the academic world. This degree is an adequate measure of education and training for most professional fields, which explains the reason students are set up to take positions in the business world when they graduate. Be that as it may, some higher positions in certain fields, for example, medicine and law may demand a postgraduate degree.

Students have the alternative of choosing from five different kinds of bachelor's degrees; they are:

Bachelor of Arts (B.A): It is viewed as the most extensive bachelor's degree.

Bachelor of Science (B.Sc.): It ordinarily embodies the majors, for example, designing, physics, accounting, Statistics, Mathematics or some other sciences.

Bachelor of Fine Arts (BFA): It is intended for singers, professional performers or actors, artists, portraitists, and other such artisans. This degree is additionally offered on platforms, for example, digital media and web design.

Bachelor of Business Administration (BBA): It extends to management courses, for example, decision making, secretarial administration, and so on.

Bachelor of Architecture (B.Arch.): It is an important degree for those who aspire to be architects.

Master's Degrees

A Master's Degree can be termed as a post graduate program runs for a period of two years. It enables students to focus on one particular field of education. Before this degree can be applied for by a student, it demands students to must have finished an undergraduate level program and most higher institutions have the least grade point requirement also, alongside an entrance examination, for example, the GRE. To have the capacity to advance effectively from a Master's degree; a capstone project or thesis is required, and it depends on the school you choose to study.

We have various kinds of Master's degrees; they are:

Master of Fine Arts (MFA) or Master of Arts (M.A.) Degree: It can cover an extensive scope of study, for example, education, communication, and social science.

Master of Science (M.Sc.): It can be obtained in a diversity of science and sociology programs.

Master of Research (M.Res.): It develops people in doing research.

Master of Philosophy (M.Phil.): It is a degree that deals with research alone and frequently provides a path to a Ph.D.

Master of Laws (LLM): It requires about two to four years to finish and offers legal advisors (lawyers) the chance to practice. Master of Business Administration (M.B.A.) is intended for the management experts with some experience.

Doctoral Degrees

Doctoral Degree is also commonly known by many as Ph.D.; this is one of the most exceptional types of degrees accessible. A few universities may expect candidates to have finished a Master's degree before proceeding to this education level while a ton of schools acknowledge individuals with Bachelor's degree also. Extra prerequisites for getting accepted into a doctoral degree program incorporate standardized test scores and letters of recommendation.

We also have various kinds of doctorate degrees; they are:

Doctor of Philosophy (Ph.D.): It is known as a research-centered doctorate program.

Specialist of Medicine (M.D): It is the highest form of degree for medical students and is a prerequisite for those who practice medicine professionally.

Specialist of Education (Ed.D.): It is the highest form of degree level in the world of academics and regularly creates a path to research.

Juris Doctor (J.D): It is a degree commonly sought after by imminent legal advisors in the United States.

We live in a world loaded with a solid challenge for employment and degrees, retaining a decent comprehension of the alternatives accessible to an individual will absolutely help a person in settling on better and well-educated decisions. It is advisable to always check each school's prerequisites and qualification criteria before opting in for any of the programs they offer (Table 2.1).

Table 2.1 Completion Time and Prerequisite per Degree Level.

[23]Degree Level	Average Completion Time (full-time)	Common Prerequisite
Associate degree	2 years	High school diploma or correspondent
Bachelor's degree	4 years	High school diploma or correspondent
Master's degree	1-2 years	Bachelor's degree
Doctoral degree	2+ years	Master's degree (sometimes bachelor's degree is acceptable)

23 "Types of Different Degree Levels" Study.com

Classification of Degrees in Various Countries

A bachelor's degree can take two forms; it's either an honors degree or an ordinary degree. Someone who doesn't meet the honors degree might be given an ordinary degree. It's all because there's a classification of degrees. Honors degree, as it is known, is usually categorized depending on the weighted average of whatever grade is achieved during the exam or some tests. Most countries have grade parameters, and it varies, but the standard and generally recognized grade value classification is listed below (Fig 6):

Figure 6 Generally Recognized Grade Value Classification.

- First Class Honors – usually 70% and above
- Second Class Honors; this takes two forms
    - a) Upper Division: ranging from 60% to 69%
    - b) Lower Division: ranging from 50% to 59%
- Third Class Honors: ranging between 40% to 49%

Many institutions in various countries adopt the use of this classification in every degree they run. They might not look exactly the way it is presented above, but an in-depth look into it will reveal it's all the same system. There is no need to give examples of countries that operates under this classification; this is a worldwide acknowledged concept.

Prerequisites for Application in Various Countries

All academic institutions in the world have different entry regulations for foreign students, it's indisputable. However, some of them share the same regulations, and it would be easy to narrow it all down. The following will discuss the requirements for admission consideration for international students in the top countries worldwide.

The United States

[24]In the United States, an individual moving to the country to run an academic program on a temporary visa, who doesn't intend to stay in the United States when done with the program and not a citizen is called an international student. They are officially labeled as a "non-resident alien" by law.

- Applicant must be prepared for the selected course of study.
- Applicant must have a satisfactory English proficiency.
- An applicant needs to prove he/she has the financial power to pay for tuition and fees for the selected course of study before being granted entry into the United States.
- Applicant must prove they have a resident at their home country where they can return to.

Institutions may request for some additional things, for example, Interviews, Recommendations, secondary courses, grade point averages, standardized test results, auditions, portfolio and sometimes, when necessary, a foreign credential evaluation.

If the foreign student meets the expected admission prerequisites and the institution is contented, a Certificate of Eligibility will be issued to the applicant.

24 "The United States Education System" World Higher Education Database (WHED)

Canada

[25]Canada runs almost the same system as the United States. Most Canadian universities tend to corresponding certificates from other nations as a requirement for entrance. They also require every applicant to possess a valid passport, apply for Visa and Student Authorization. Applicants must be skilled in French or English language.

[26]The academic record of the applicant is very crucial because of the huge competition with admission consideration. Proof of academic credentials will be requested from the applicant, and they could be;

- Comprehensive course outline.
- Degree Certificate(s) or Diploma(s).
- Transcript.

For applicants from a foreign country whose documents are in a different language other than French or English, there might be a need for an authorized translation. The institution might need to evaluate the applicant's past academic credentials to:

- Validate the legitimacy of the documents.
- Juxtapose students with credentials that were issued from a region close or within Canada.
- If applicable, grant transfer credits.

Like the United States, every institution in the country has solitary rights to define the acknowledgment of the academic credentials of the applicant to determine admission considerations.

---

25 "Canada Education System" World Higher Education Database (WHED)
26 "Information on admission requirements" The Canadian Information Centre for International Credentials.

India

[27]Almost all institutions in India have platforms for foreign students so as to make it easier for them to move to India. There are also various Education Consultants set up by the government to attend to the needs of the increasing number of foreign students.

There are numerous courses that foreign student can apply for in the country. However, they are required to submit some important documents, such as, residence permit, admission letter, passport, etc. before admission can be considered. An applicant may take advantage of the residential permit if they register at the Foreigners' Registration Office not longer than a week after their arrival. India institutions requirements for foreign students are similar to other countries, but they give major attention to the qualifications the applicant is presenting, although various institutions have their scale of measurement for qualifications. Some of the major prerequisites are English Language proficiency, an entry and a passport that is valid for at least six months.

Japan

[28]n Japan, every institution requires a minimum of one round of exams before consideration for admission. The top institution in Japan, University of Tokyo, carries out a lot of exams so as to filter out student with low scores or who can't keep up with the system, and creates a platform for capable applicants.

Japanese institution programs are not nearly as tough as their exams taken for admissions consideration. But, most applicants encounter no problem finishing their degree after being admitted

27 "Study in India" educations.com
28 "Entering Japanese university" justlanded.com

into the institution. Before being considered for admission, foreign applicants must meet the following requirements:

- Own a valid passport.
- Show that you are financially capable of paying every expense while studying.
- Must have Japanese language proficiency (this is not compulsorily a requirement; however, an applicant might tussle in the course of study if there is no basic knowledge of the language).
- Recommendation from a teacher or professor.
- Passport-size photographs.
- Diploma(s) or High School transcript.

International students find it convenient getting admitted into Japanese institutions, the primary reason for this is that the government inspires an interracial university population. However, an applicant shouldn't assume application without entrance exam; although a foreign student is not put through the excruciating Japanese exams, it is necessary to go through the exam prepared for foreign students by the Japanese University Admission. This involves academic and language testing, it is carried out two times in a year; summer and fall. The applicant might also need to apply for a Test of English as a Foreign Language, known as TOEFL if he/she is not a native English speaker and the institution being applied to demands for such skill.

Australia

[29]Institutions in Australia are quite straightforward with their demands for international students. There are tests to take, and there are documents to submit. Since there is a considerable need for language proficiency, a language test is carried out and

29 "How to Apply to an International University in Australia in 2019" Ana-Maria Pasolea

the following language proficiency test they accept for foreign students:

- C1 Advanced
- IELTS
- TOEFL
- Pearson Test of English (PTE)
- Victorian Certificate of Education (VCE)

Note that it is not every country that is required to tender this English Language test certificates, an applicant should carry out a proper check to know if he/she is exempted from the list or not.

There are also some documents required to be submitted before being considered for admission; they are as follows:

- Official Academic Transcripts
- Certificate of Award.
- Personal details.
- Proof of level of English Language proficiency with the certificate.

Other additional requirements are:

- Official proof for a name change (if there is a change of name)
- Final grades (if you applied to the institution prior to your final exams)
- Official translations of documents (if they are not in English language)

Every institution in Australia has distinct closing dates for application; therefore it rests on the applicant to research and discover the exact dates to apply. Nevertheless, the general application periods are as follow:

- October ending to Middle of November: First semester application period.
- Middle of April to Middle of May: Second semester application period.

Challenges and Complications with Various Countries

Challenges and complications should be expected when education is involved and also in a foreign country. We have so many institutions in the world with problems, so this section will discuss the general challenges and complications known to be encountered worldwide. It can be a very challenging experience for a foreign student being the first time of application.

[30]It can be challenging when strangers you have no acquaintance with peruse your application, and they will assess you based on your previous academic performance, but not only that, they will also evaluate professionalism and interest.

During the admission process, there are some things foreign students face that they could have tackled easily if only they knew just what to do at that moment. Some of the challenges that many foreign students encounter when processing their admission are as follow:

- **Difficulty paying processing fee:** Most institutions in countries around the world expect students to pay certain amount of money for the application alone. This is reasonable, in the sense that those evaluating credentials devote a large portion of their time perusing applications. Nevertheless, for any foreign student under a monetary burden, in dire need of financial help, and also attempting to process a number of institutions, finance can pose to be a significant barrier. Some institutions offer a service called "fee waiver" for the students who are having difficulty paying their application fees. Be hopeful and have in mind that it might just turn out you don't need to pay a dime for the application.

30 "College Application Challenges" U.S. News & World Report.

- **Composing additional essays:** Many institutions demand that foreign students write an extra essay about what makes them distinct and also to demonstrate their interest. Although these essay could prove to be an excellent opportunity for students to demonstrate their characterizing potentials, they go through the worries of including due dates, spending a lot of time proofreading and the pressure of it, all these could be particularly demanding for foreign students whose native or first language is different from English.

Notwithstanding the additional pressure, these essays merit your time and vitality. If you begin early, you will discover gradually that you are putting more exertion into them, and the chances that you will get into your desired school will increase.

- **Scholarship Application:** Money is a critical factor for processing admission into a foreign institution. Many foreign students struggle to limit their school costs by however much they could. They carry this out by presenting their essays and reaching out to every association that offers a scholarship. In the process of doing this, they get carried away and forget the fact that they are keeping their eyes off the primary assignment; admission into college. As a foreign student, you shouldn't exhaust too much time focusing your attention on so many things and spending little time on the essays given by the college and other reports, doing so will throw you off balance. It is advisable to always stick to the main objective.

- **Picking between college applications and final exams:** In many countries where their institutions trail a calendar for semester, there will probably be an early conclusion of application due dates, and their last, most important tests will clash on the same day. This leaves the students in a bad spot; they battle with the question of whether they should invest most of their energy and time getting ready for their applications and give less attention to the final exams, or the other way round. You have to realize that getting good grades maximizes your chance of being admitted into a college; you need your grades!

Chapter Three
Countries' Educational System

In this chapter, the five major factors that are used during academic evaluation in foreign countries will be extensively discussed. Much description will be made on each factor so that applicants will know how their credentials will be arbitrated.

Moreover, there is an international body that takes care of educational systems across all higher institutions in the world; it is called the World Higher Education Database (WHED). [31]WHED is an International Association of Universities' (IAU) exclusive online reference platform which offers detailed and inclusive information on Institutions, Credentials, and Higher Educations Systems everywhere in the world. WHED also supplies official and reliable information on higher education globally. IAU secretariat obtains and keeps information up to date in the WHED every now and then, concentrating on a particular region each year. They carry this out in conjunction with UNESCO.

The five factors that are considered during international academic evaluations are; the level of education, the completion period, the field of specialization, the authenticity of the previously attended institution, nature and duration of course.

---

31 "UNESCO – World Higher Education Database" https://www.iau-aiu.net/World-Higher-Education-Database-WHED

Level of Education

Many people like to believe their home country's phase of education is the most legitimate in the world. While that might be true, a student who plans to study beyond the horizon of his/her home country shouldn't have that mentality. Different countries around the world have their distinct educational system, and any international student wishing to study in a country has to know about the system before applying for admission. The level of education doesn't depend on individual institutions in a country; it is the federal ministry of education that decides that. That means a country can't incorporate more than one educational system.

The level of education varies according to countries, which will be too large a study to discuss. The generally known and accepted levels of education would be considered, and example of countries that run it would be given. The world has two stages of education in common; the Primary education and Secondary education. Although there are many subcategories under these two, they are still the basic educational set up for any country.

Primary Education

[32]Primary Education can be termed as the preliminary phase of education. The general purpose of primary education is to set up a platform to educate children, without the consideration of country of origin, gender, or age, to accomplish a decent intellectual, passionate and mental development, and enhancement. This level of education is mandatory for every kid; it is the first stage of formal education. Some countries call it elementary school and it's divided into sub-levels like;

32 "Strategic Direction: National Association for the Education of Young Children." naeyc.org.

grade 1, grade 2, etc. In most countries, the middle school follows primary education. For example, primary school education runs from Grade one to three in the United States and elementary school is from grade one to six. Australia too runs their primary education from Grade one to six. Every country with an educational system has a primary education platform; the only difference is how they classify them.

Secondary Education

This form of education is divided into two stages; the upper or senior secondary education and the lower or junior secondary education. Secondary education ordinarily happens following six years of primary education. It is also called higher education in many nations. Secondary education is mandatory in every country just like primary education. The least required age before secondary education in many countries is 16. It is also the final phase of all mandatory education in most countries.

Tertiary Education

[33]Tertiary education is any form of education that goes beyond the secondary (high) school level. Certificates or degrees acquired under tertiary education includes; Diplomas, Associate's degree, Graduate and Undergraduate degrees, Bachelor's degree, Master's degree, and doctorate. It is popularly also termed as postsecondary education or third-phase of education. It takes around four years to complete in most countries. Universities and Colleges fall under the category of Tertiary institutions. Qualifications attained from previous institutions attended are mostly used in this level of education to further one's academic career. This is regarded as

33 "What Is Tertiary Education?" Learn.org

the highest form of education, but there are other professional educations that one pursues after completing this level. These professional educations are not available in every country because most of them are carried out by external bodies.

Completion Period

Completion period or length of study can't be measured based on a degree because each course of study has its time span and they vary. The following tables (3.1-3.5) shows the completion period of the most common degrees attainable in different countries:

Table 3.1 Length of Different Bachelor's Degrees.

[34]**Bachelor's Degree (Within the period of 3 to 4 years)**	
DEGREE	**PERIOD**
Bachelor's Degree in Arts in Study and Career Guidance	3 years
Bachelor's Degree in Science in Audiology	3 years
Bachelor's Degree in Science in Biomedical Laboratory Science	3 years
Bachelor's Degree in Science in Dental Technology	3 years
Bachelor's Degree in Science in Diagnostic Radiology Nursing	3 years
Bachelor's Degree in Science in Dietetics	3 years
Bachelor's Degree in Science in Engineering	3 years
Bachelor's Degree in Science in Forest Management	3 years
Bachelor's Degree in Science in Landscape Construction and Management	3 years
Bachelor's Degree in Science in Marine Engineering	3 years
Bachelor's Degree in Science in Nautical Science	3 years
Bachelor's Degree in Science in Nursing	3 years
Bachelor's Degree in Science in Occupational Therapy	3 years
Bachelor's Degree in Science in Optometry	3 years
Bachelor's Degree in Science in Pharmacy	3 years

34 "Study levels and degrees" Swedish Council for Higher Education

Bachelor's Degree in Science in Physiotherapy	3 years
Bachelor's Degree in Science in Prosthetics and Orthotics	3 years
Bachelor's Degree in Preschool Teaching	3.5 years
Bachelor's Degree in Science in Fire Protection Engineering	3.5 years
Bachelor's Degree in Science in Social Work	3.5 years

Table 3.2 Length of Different Higher Level Diplomas.

Higher National Diploma (Within the period of 1 to 2 years)	
DEGREE	**PERIOD**
Higher Education Diploma in Folk High School Education	1 year
Higher Education Diploma in Vocational Education	1.5 years
Higher Education Diploma in Agricultural & Rural Management	2 years
Higher Education Diploma in Dental Hygiene	2 years
Higher Education Diploma in Equine Science	2 years
Higher Education Diploma in Forest Management	2 years
Higher Education Diploma in Horticultural Management	2 years
Higher Education Diploma in Veterinary Nursing	2 years

Table 3.3 Length of Different Master's Degrees.

Master's Degree (Within the period of 1 to 6 years)	
DEGREE	**PERIOD**
Master's Degree in Arts in Primary Education	4 years
Master's Degree in Science in Speech and Language Pathology	4 years
Master's Degree in Laws	4.5 years
Master's Degree in Science in Agriculture	4.5 years
Master's Degree in Arts/Science in Secondary Education, Master's Degree in Arts/Science in Upper Secondary Education (Subject teacher)	4.5/5/5.5 years
Master's Degree in Architecture	5 years
Master's Degree in Science in Business and Economics	5 years
Master's Degree in Science in Dental Surgery	5 years
Master's Degree in Science in Engineering	5 years
Master's Degree in Science in Forestry	5 years
Master's Degree in Science in Horticulture	5 years
Master's Degree in Science in Landscape Architecture	5 years

Master's Degree in Science in Medical Physics	5 years
Master's Degree in Science in Pharmacy	5 years
Master's Degree in Science in Psychology	5 years
Master's Degree in Science in Medicine	5.5 years
Master's Degree in Science in Veterinary Medicine	5.5 years

Table 3.4 Length of Different Post Graduate Diplomas.

Postgraduate Diploma (Within the period of 1 to 2 year(s))	
DEGREE	**PERIOD**
Postgraduate Diploma in Midwifery (Bachelor of Science in professional status qualification and Nursing required)	1.5 years
Postgraduate Diploma in Psychotherapy (Master of Science in Medicine with specific specialization, Master of Science in Psychology, Bachelor of Science in Social Work or the correspondent required)	1.5 years
Postgraduate Diploma in Specialist Nursing (Bachelor of Science in professional status qualification and Nursing required)	1 year, 1.25 years for specialization in district nursing
Postgraduate Diploma in Special Educational Needs (Bachelor of Arts in Education required)	1.5 years

Table 3.5 Length of Different Doctoral Degrees.

Doctorate (Within the period of 2 to 4 years)	
DEGREE	**PERIOD**
Licentiate's Degree	4.5 years
Doctor's Degree	5 years

The above tables do not contain all obtainable degree but as a representative of other similar degrees and the length parameter for each of them.

Field of Specialization

Credential evaluators give importance to the field of specialization of an international student. It is based on career goals, skills, and personality. The course studied by an applicant in his/her previously attended institution will be compared with the aspired course of study in the foreign country. The chosen course should have relativity to the previously studied course. Also, many courses offered in an institution can have many specializations beneath it. A particular course might be available in the applicant's home country and unavailable in the foreign country, therefore the applicant must choose a course that is within the field of specialization of the desired course of study.

Most institutions tend to always give an entrance test based on the field of specialization because the candidate might not have studied the same course in his/her previously attended institution. The idea is to make things easier for the applicant when being considered for admission so he/she wouldn't fail the entrance examination without a fair trial. The examination will be dependent on the field of specialization. Many applicants fail to acknowledge their field of specialization when applying to an overseas institution, especially when they register through an online platform. Thus, it makes the entrance examination difficult, and they would later be denied admission. International students also must choose courses that will give them a deep and extensive understanding of the chosen field of specialization. Specialization deepens the understanding of any chosen area of study. It makes an individual focus on the degree being pursued and the intended career path after completion.

[35]There are some international students with no prior educational attainment who have intentions of obtaining a

35 "Fields of Specialization" ECE ILLINOIS

degree pertaining to a particular field of specialization but not focusing on which course would be suitable for them. They usually devote most of their time getting the elementary concept of the chosen field. However, they encounter problems when it comes to selecting courses after they have already decided on a desired field of specialization. This category of international students ends up acknowledging all the listed courses as needed and then picks at random. Credential evaluators take their time to assess the aspect of the field of specialization of an applicant when evaluating credentials; it is worthy of taking note of.

Authenticity of Antecedent Institution

A credential from a foreign country can't be legitimately assessed without considering the authenticity of the institution that is awarding the credential. Many credentials evaluating services have a strong requirement that the all credentials being submitted must be from an institution that is authorized to award certificates or credentials that are professionally and academically acceptable in the nation of origin. Additionally, all the programs must be accredited.

[36]A credential is assumed to be a suitable minimum educational level in a specific country if the institution or the program is accredited and recognized. Varying terms might be utilized to portray the status of a program or an institution in every nation. There are two words known to be used for validation of an institution or program; accreditation and recognition. Most people would say they have the same meaning, but they are not equivalent words.

Accreditation is an official pronouncement by an acknowledged authority which has assessed and validate if a program, as well as the institution, meet the laid-down minimum quality principles. Accreditation is typically a non-mandatory procedure and is only valid for a predetermined number of years. It is expected that the accreditation of a program or an institution should be renewed when it expires. The reason there could be differences in the manner in which a program or an institution is accredited in various countries could be the level of involvement of government or how voluntary the process is. The acknowledgment of credentials in many countries relies upon whether the program or institution is accredited; therefore, it is in a way mandatory for all institutions.

36 "Quality assurance: accredited programmes" Enic-Naric

Recognition, on the other hand, is an authorized status approved by national legislation. Institutions that satisfy the prerequisites fixed in federal legislation and possess an authority that grants degree are known to be recognized institutions.

In certain nations, a temporary permit is granted to institutions to function as an educational body. It is done for a period of time so the decision to be made would be under review. Permitting isn't proportionate to accreditation, and it does not demand exhibition of value. An authorized institution needs to pass through the process of accreditation before being accredited. The institution has the privilege to officially award recognized credentials only when it has been accredited. It is then that it also has public funding access.

When discussing the accreditation and recognition of programs and institution, quality affirmation is also a factor. In higher education, quality assurance consists of practices, policies, and processes that are intended to accomplish, manage and improve the nature of the institution as well as the program.

Credentials that are awarded by a recognized institution are generally accepted to be recognized. But in certain nations, there is a difference between the accreditation or recognition of an institution and accreditation or recognition of a program. That is, it is likely that a recognized institution offers officially unrecognized programs and also that an unrecognized institution offers a recognized program. Verification is always done by credential evaluation agencies to ascertain the accreditation and recognition of a program or status of an institution that awards a qualification to know if the program or institution has a place in the educational system of a particular nation. [37]Certification evaluation agencies like WES also depend on accreditation bodies for quality assurance as proof that a program or an institution conforms to the least quality principle of a given country.

37 "Understanding the WES Evaluation Process" WES

Nature and Duration of Course

This matters a lot when a credential evaluation is being done. Some programs are complicated than others. There are different criteria for admission according to programs. The nature of the program and the period taken to pursue it determine a lot during evaluation. The following points are the effect of the nature and longevity of course in credential evaluation.

- The longer the time taken to evaluate the course of study, the more the evaluating agency charges the applicant.
- The level of the course determines the complexity of the entrance requirements.
- Some courses require that the applicants should be called upon for an interview.

Chapter Four
Grading System And Measurement

The Carnegie Unit

Some institutions call it "The Carnegie Hour," but they both have a standard definition. The Carnegie unit is an estimate of the time duration that a student uses to study a subject. Students get credit awards for classes based on the Carnegie unit.

[38]It both ensures and systemizes the standard of high school education. Many people have criticized it as an obstacle to flexibility. However, irrespective of its confinements, the Carnegie unit continues to assure that students merit the credit for all the time they invest in every course.

[39]Carnegie Unit solves the problem of not knowing how much knowledge is gained from each course with the time spent studying it. It merely compares seat-time with knowledge gained. Each unit of a Carnegie represents around 130 teaching hours. A unit is mostly referred to as a course that holds each day at school for a period of 50 minutes to 55 minutes. The Carnegie unit always inspires a lot of things that are essential for teaching

38 "Carnegie Units" Stateuniversity.com
39 "The Carnegie Unit – Revisited" Elena Silva

and learning in institutions. It influences the school year and the school day, the longevity of a class period and also the time spent to be awarded a degree. The Carnegie unit transforms the method that learning is being organized for educational reasons. Therefore, suppressing all form of integrative teaching carried out because of the difficulty of questions about making a decision of the number of units to be allocated to individual discipline. Although most critics believe that time taken to sit and learn is not a determiner for the knowledge attained in schools and secondary institutions should be pliable to undertake students and enhance education. Using a timetable or block schedule demands that a course should run for a designated number of hours. However, the number of hours may differ from that of conventional courses, for the reason that the method used for time arrangement might differ.

When it comes to evaluation, the Carnegie unit is mostly used when course by course method is being used. Carnegie Foundation for the Advancement of Teaching initiated the Carnegie unit, named after the originator, Andrew Carnegie. We also have the Carnegie Classification; most institutions have their various categories. It is being classified based on the profile of the institutions like kinds of degree offered, specialization, and the academic courses offered. The importance of the classification is to show the uniqueness of each institution. It does not at any point meant to be a rating scale of any institution. Many new systems are being introduced into the education framework. Many institutions now have interests in considering changing the method by which they weigh student learning. However, as of now, the Carnegie Unit is still the most stabilized he and commonly used method of evaluation since other measures available have not been tested and trusted. There are unrequired questions, about which method will prove to work best, which type of institution it will be suitable for and under what conditions. If the method of credential evaluation to be used by evaluation agencies is the course by course method, the Carnegie Unit is still the most considered technique.

Currently, the Carnegie Unit is the keystone to the management of many higher education institutions. It also serves as a means of providing the ability to conduct and compare institutions, students and faculties. The Carnegie unit remains to be the standard for evaluating the entry of students into various institutions.

Contact Hours

A contact hour is a time measurement in which a student is involved in a lecture or a teaching section with a lecturer or teacher. A contact hour is equivalent to 50 minutes.

A credit hour is a unit that measures the course work done in an institution.

The difference between contact hour and credit hour is that a student obtains credit hour depending on the amount of contact hours spent during a study in class in a week.

A credit hour is usually awarded for an adequate achievement of a period of 50-minutes in a classroom lecture in a week throughout a semester of at least 15 weeks. Institutions may modify the initial measurement symmetrically so as to fit into an adjusted format of study and academic calendars.

[40]A credit hour consists of an average input of 3 hours in a week for every student, leaving an hour two for out-of-class or field experiences. The amount of credit hours attached to a course shows, in a quantitative format, the expected outcome, amount of time spent in the classroom, the form of learning, and the expected total of external elementary work for a class. There is an apparent variation between the measurements of credit hour in institutions. Many institutions have a steady and stable measurement for contact hour and credit hour for courses they offer, which makes it possible and easy for credential evaluation agencies to compare different programs from various institutions. This makes it easier for universities and colleges to give out transcripts that are acceptable and gives full expression and impression of a student's academic performance. [41]Most institutions grade set their tuition fee making use of Semester

40 "Semester Credit Hours Guidelines" purdue.edu

41 "What You Need to Know about Academic Credit Systems in the U.S." Alexandru Pop

Credit Hours for applicants. Depending on the institution, international students need to take credit hours ranging from 9 to 12 hours in a semester. The overall score for every course and their credit hours allotted to them by the program being studied determines a student's semester GPA.

When a credential evaluation is being carried out on a foreign credential, contact hour is used as one of the points of reference regarding academic studies. This leads to the weighing and conversion of courses to semester credits is carried out and also where GPA is finally calculated. If you're planning to become an international student, it's imperial for you to research on how credits are awarded and converted at your choice of institution.

Length and Conversion of Semester and Quarter

There are so many distinct ways of earning a degree in an institution. Foreign transfer students often find credit transferring into a new institution confusing sometimes. This occurs mostly when the credit transfer is being done between two different institutions with different academic frameworks.

To maintain a strategic distance from the confusion of how to transfer credits from a quarter system to a semester system or the other way around, there are a couple of things you have to be acquainted with so as to start again smoothly and obtain your degree. Higher education institutions usually utilize one of two basic systems to organize classes and grant credit all through the quarters and semesters, i.e., the whole year.

In a quarter framework, students commonly go to classes for 4 quarters every year, regularly all year. The length of a quarter often differs in length, but averagely, a quarter should run for around 10 to 11 weeks.

On the other hand, in semester frameworks, students ordinarily go to classes for two semesters every year; they are called "fall semester" and "spring semester." The length of the semesters, however, can likewise fluctuate.

The quarter system and semester system permit students to complete their degree in about two to four years. It is dependent on the nature of courses taken, the program being studied and the institution itself. The number of awarded credits might vary among the two educational systems because of the differences in both schemes. The difference between both systems usually creates much confusion when the credit transfer process is being done.

Credit Conversion

If you are changing into any of the two educational systems that is entirely different from the system used at your previously attended institution, there is a need for conversion of your credits to match the new institution credit prerequisites.

[42]Despite the fact that there is generally accepted conversion scale for institutions, every institution has a right to choose the way they convert their credits, but the rate of conversion should not go far from the conversion rate generally known to be used. The review and conversion of an applicant's credits are up to the institution the applicant is transferring to so as to decide the measure of credits the candidate would be granted after being accepted into their system.

It is important for the applicant to know that when credit conversion is being done, it might seem that credits are being gained when transferring from a quarter system into a semester system or lost when you are transferring from a semester system into a quarter system. Nevertheless, the total sum of credits required to be awarded a degree will likewise be different between the systems. Moreover, there is a conversion ration that has been created to guarantee a genuinely smooth method of transferring your credits between the quarter system and semester system.

Transferring credit is a clever way of saving money and time. If you are a foreign student preparing to get your education transferred, go to your previously attended institution and request for a copy of your transcripts and start studying the policies and procedures of credit transfer with someone in the new institution that has adequate knowledge of it. The time taken to complete your degree will also be dependent on the measure of credit

---

42 "Semester vs. Quarter: What You Need to Know When Transferring Credits" Grant Tilus

accepted. Many institutions may have a varying review for your credits; therefore, try to discover an institution that best converts your credits towards completing your degree.

Various Grading Scales

[43]In education, grading can be defined as the application of systematized techniques of measurement of different stages of accomplishment in a course. Letters can be used to represent grades, most educational institutions use A to F. Some institutions use 1 to 6 as range, and some use a percentage format. In certain nations, the average of every grade from every course is used to generate a grade point average called GPA for the marking time frame. [44]The grade point average (GPA) is determined by using the grade points earned by a student at a particular point of time during middle school in high school. It is also used for calculation for both graduate and undergraduate students in many institutions. Employers, Universities, and Colleges around the world also make use of GPA to evaluate and weigh applicants.

There is also a cumulative grade point average called CGPA. It is a computation of the average grade of the total points earned by each student and divided by the practicable overall number of points. This grading system measures the student education career. GPAs can be weighted or unweighted. Weighted grade point average is where some courses are rated higher than other courses, and unweighted grade point average is where every course that shares similar credit numbers has the same impact on the grade point average (GPA).

---

43 "Il liceale con la media del 9,93 "Sono il più bravo d'Italia." Repubblica .it

44 "Grade Point Average" dictionary.reference

Various countries have their grading scales and although their grading may be similar, the format may not be. Below are the grading scales of some top countries in the world.

The United States

[45]Many institutions in the United States award grades in letters, F to A, for every course taken. The overall Grade Point Average is then determined by these letters. The GPA ranges from 1.0 to 4.0 respectively, and it is computed by using a specific formula. In the US, private institutions use 3.3 as their GPA average, and public institutions use 3.0 as their GPA average. Table 4.1 shows the most commonly used grading system in the United States:

Table 4.1 Commonly Used Grading System in the US.

Grade symbol	Percentage	GPA
A	90%-100%	4.0
B	80%-89%	3.0
C	74%-79%	2.0
D	70%-73%	1.0
F	0%-69%	0.0

45 "Want a Higher GPA, Go to a Private College" Rampell Catherine.

Table 4.2 is the breakdown of the grading system used in the United States by many institutions, but not all:

Table 4.2 Breakdown of Grading System.

[46]Grade symbol	Percentage	GPA
A+	97–100%	4.33/4.00 or 4.00/4.00
A	93–96%	4.00/4.00
A−	90–92%	3.67/4.00
B+	87–89%	3.33/4.00
B	83–86%	3.00/4.00
B−	80–82%	2.67/4.00
C+	77–79%	2.33/4.00
C	73–76%	2.00/4.00
C-	70–72%	1.67/4.00
D+	67–69%	1.33/4.00
D	63–66%	1.00/4.00
D-	60–62%	0.67/4.00
F	0–59%	0.00/4.00

Canada

[47]In Canada, individual regions are permitted to fabricate their grading systems. Therefore, the academic grading differs by level of education, province, faculty, and institution (Tables 4.3-4.6). Since there are various scales from all regions, the following will discuss only five grading systems in various countries.

46 "International Grade Equivalencies" unco.edu
47 "Grading System in Canada" Ana-Maria Pasolea

Ontario

Table 4.3 Grades Breakdown: Ontario.

[48]Symbol	Percentage
A+	95%–100%
A	87%–94%
A-	80%–86%
B+	77%–79%
B	73%–76%
B-	70%–72%
C+	67%–69%
C	63%–66%
C-	60%–62%
D+	57%–59%
D	53%–56%
D-	50%–52%
R	0%–49%

Grade interpretation:

- A - Level 4 (Above government standards)
- B - Level 3 (Government standards)
- C - Level 2 (Almost government standards)
- D - Level 1 (Below government standards)
- R - No Level (Remedial standards)
- F - No Level (Failing standards)

48 http://www.edu.gov.on.ca/eng/policyfunding/growsuccess.pdf#page=46

[49]Quebec

Table 4.4 Grades Breakdown: Quebec

Grade symbol	**Percent**
A	86%–100%
B	73%–85%
C+	67%–72%
C	60%–66%
C-	0%-59%
F	0%–0%

A = Outstanding and excellent performance.

B = Very good performance.

C+ = Good performance.

C = Satisfactory performance.

C- = Minimally acceptable performance.

I = Below minimally acceptable performance. (Incomplete)

F= Failed (This can be used as a concluding grade if the “I” (Incomplete)grade has been assigned before or if “F” is given because of failure in a course exam that is regional.

W = Withdrawal.

SG = Standing Granted.

TS = Transfer Standing.

49 http://www2.gov.bc.ca/DownloadAsset?assetId=8CE360A6A6DF748388381677

Alberta

Table 4.5 Grades Breakdown: Alberta.

Symbol	Percentage
A+	90%–100%
A	85%–89%
A-	80%–84%
B+	75%–79%
B	70%–74%
B-	65%–69%
C+	60%–64%
C	56%–59%
C-	50%–55%
D	0%–49%

Grade Interpretation:

A = 80% - 100% (Outstanding performance)

B = 65% - 79% (Brilliant performance)

C = 50% - 64% (Adequate performance)

D = 0% - 49% (Limited performance)

British Columbia

Table 4.6 Grades Breakdown: British Columbia

Letter	Percentage
A	86%–100%
B	73%–85%
C+	67%–72%
C	60%–66%
C-	50%–59%
F	0%–49%
I	0%–49%
W	Withdrawn
P	Pass

Grade Interpretation:

A = Excellent performance.

B = Very good performance.

C+ = Good performance.

C = Satisfactory performance.

C- = Minimally acceptable performance.

F = Fail (Below 50%)

I = Incomplete

W = Withdrawn (This happens when a student withdraws from a course)

P = Pass (Although no grade is available for this, the student is labeled to have passed, this happens when a student is switching grading systems or institutions)

[50]Australia

There are diverse grading systems in Australia; it varies according to the level of education. However, our major concern is the tertiary institutions' grading systems. There are only two grading systems known to be used by tertiary institutions in Australia (Tables 4.7-4.8). They are as follow:

1. Grading System 1

Table 4.7 Grading System 1: Australia

Symbol	Percentage
HD	80% and above (High Distinction)
D	70–79% (Distinction)
Cr	60–69% (Credit)
P	50–59% (Pass)
F	49% and under (Fail)

2. Grading System 2

Table 4.8 Grading System 2: Australia

Symbol	Percentage
H1	80% and above (First Class Honors)
H2A	75–79% (Second Class Honors (A Division))
H2B	70–74% (Second Class Honors (B Division))
H3	65–69% (Third Class Honors)
P	50–64% (Pass)
F	below 50% (Fail)

50 "8 University Grading Systems Around the World that May or May Not Be Weird" Ana-Maria Pasolea

In most institutions in the country, GPA is computed with the following:

High Distinction: 4.0
Distinction: 3.0
Credit: 2.0
Pass: 1.0

India

Indian Institutes of Technology run a 10-point Grading System while Universities run a Percentage Grading System. The maximum mark is 100, and the minimum is 0, required pass mark for all students ranges from 30 to 40 depending on the institution (Tables 4.9-4.10).

Table 4.9 Grades Classification in India.

Classification/Division	Percentage
75% and above	Distinction
60% to 74%	First Class
50% to 59%	Second Class
35% (or 40%) to 49%	Pass
39% (or 34%) below	Fail

Few institutions in India consider a lower percentage as pass.

Table 4.10 Grades Point and Description.

Grade Symbol	Grade Points	Grade
S	9–10	Excellent (top students)
A	8–9	Very good
B	7–8	Good
C	6–7	Satisfactory Work
D	4–6	Sufficient (passed)
E	3–4	Not Sufficient (not passed)
U	0	Unfair Behavior (cheating)

Table 4.11 shows the international conversion of grades developed by World Education Services (WES) for percentages scored in Institutions in India.

Table 4.11 International Conversion of Grades by WES.

Classification/Division	[51]**Percentage**	**The United States Grade Equivalent**	**Grade Point**
First class/Distinction/Outstanding	60% – 100%	A or (O)	3.5 – 4.0
Second Class (Upper Division)	55% – 59%	B+	3.15 – 3.49
Second Class (Lower Division)	50% – 54%	B	2.5 – 3.14
Third Division	43% – 49%	C+	2.15 – 2.49
Fail or third division	35% – 42%	C	1.5 – 2.14
Fail	0 – 34%	F	0 – 1.49

Few institutions in India consider a lower percentage as pass.

51 "WES Grade Conversion Guide." World Education Services

The United Kingdom

In the United Kingdom, they award a degree with or without honors. The weighted average mark of the work of the student being evaluated is used to determine the class of an honors degree to be awarded. They classify the degree according to the following:

- 1st - First class honors
- 2.1 - Second class honors (Upper division)
- 2.2 - Second class honors (Lower division)
- 3rd - Third class honors
- Pass (Ordinary degree)

Note that not all grading systems are the same in the United Kingdom. The European academic grading system is quite different from this. However, they all make use of the British undergraduate degree classification system.

With all these grading systems listed above, a foreign student should have an idea about how grading systems look like internationally. It is advisable for an applicant to research thoroughly on the grading system of their institution of choice.

System Conversions Across Countries

In this division, step-by-step directives on how to calculate a grade point average for admission and other educational reasons. Additionally, it will explain how to go about the conversion of grades from international transcripts, thereby making foreign degrees to be easy to assess by making use of the GPA procedure about to be discussed. It is important for you to know ways of calculating your grade point average (GPA) and your cumulative grade point average (CGPA). It prepares you to set and plan your academic goals, and it will set you on the right path to success.

[52]GPA Calculation & International Grade Conversion

The following contains the list of requirements to convert and calculate GPA:

1. **Transcripts:** Transcripts will be required to work on the GPA computation. If the entire transcripts are not available yet, hold on till you have it all in your possession before you start the calculation.
2. **A CGPA Calculator:** There are so many CGPA computing software and organizations in the world. Nevertheless, it is advisable to find the perfect one to use for calculating your GPA. One of the best and recommended organizations you can make use of their CGPA calculator is World Education Services (WES).

[53]World Education Services is one of the best places to visit if you are planning to calculate any GPA. It is one of the best and commonly known organizations that deal with credential evaluations and GPA calculation. They invented international grade point average calculator, popularly known as the iGPA calculator. This computes and compares your grades to the 4.0

52 "GPA Calculation & International Grade Conversion" McGill University
53 "iGPA Calculator" World Education Services

grading measure in the United States. Your GPA conversion will be based on the general grading scale used in the country you obtained the transcripts. All that is required are your transcripts and marksheets. Before you can use iGPA; you need to have your grades ready. You can assess their website by clicking this link: http://www.wes.org/students/igpacalc.asp

3. **International Degree Equivalency Fact Sheets (Idefs):** This will only be needed for consult if an applicant possesses a transcript that is issued from an institution from a country outside the United States or Canada.

[54]Sadly, there exists no generally accepted or universal technique of calculating GPA. This is because methods differ by institution and by country. Some institutions weigh marks by units or award additional points for honors classes. Basically, the things you need to calculate your GPA is to find a grading scale, convert or translate every grade letter to an equivalent numerical or quantitative value. After that, find the average of the values to get your GPA. If you have any scores that are weighted, you may need to do additional calculations. Visit the following sites if you need to convert your grades, or you want to know academic information about your country to the United States grade scale:

https://www.scholaro.com/grade-conversion,https://applications.wes.org/country-resources/resources.asp.

54 "How to Calculate GPA" Rachel Scoggins

Chapter Five

Validations and Qualification Frameworks

Roles of an Applicant

We discussed a lot about the credential evaluation agencies, processes, grades scales, institutions, mode of entries and so many more in the previous chapters. The section will be fully dedicated to the responsibilities of a foreign applicant. With the information so far in this book, the reader should have a basic knowledge of what academic credential evaluation is and the different systems used in various countries. This final chapter of the book is to guide the applicant on the parts they have to play to become an international student.

These responsibilities are divided into three categories; **Before the application, During the application, and After the application.**

Before The Application

As a foreign aspirant, there are so many preparations and research you have to do to make yourself ready to start the journey. They are as follow (Fig 7):

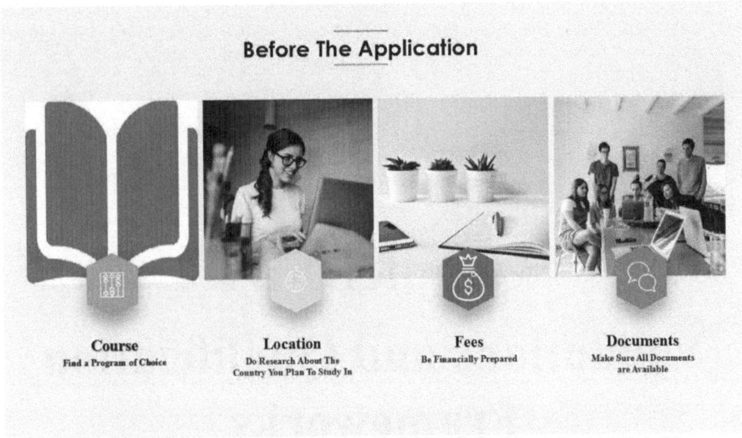

Figure 7 Roles of an Applicant: Before the Application.

- [55]**Find A Program Of Choice:** Once you have determined in your mind to study in a foreign country, the next step to take is to start research immediately. Browse online for different programs, read their reviews, choose your desired program, do significant research on the program to know if you are fit for it and if it is what you truly want and not some fancy program that sounds cool. You can discuss it with someone close to you, your parent, guardian, friends, etc. Get a program advisor and affirm your credit transfer.
- [56]**Do Research About The Country You Plan To Study**: Familiarize yourself with the country you are planning to study. Get to know their culture, the people, the weather, the economy, cost of living, prices of things compared to your home country. Knowing all these things will enhance your experience. Since you are planning to

55 "10 Step How-To Guide on Preparing to Study Abroad" Kali Slaymaker
56 How Should I Prepare to Study Abroad?" greatvaluecollege.net

spend at least a year to study in a foreign country, make sure you pre-plan well to enjoy your stay throughout the study period.

- [57]**Be Financially Prepared:** The next step is to sit down and evaluate your financial capability. Be certain that you have sufficient money to settle some expenses like; application expenses, trip expenses (Visa and Passport), study expenses, accommodation and feeding expenses, etc. You may probably find out that you will be spending much money than you imagined. Be mindful of your financial status so you won't get stuck at a point. You may even apply for a scholarship or financial aid; there are many agencies like that in the world.
- [58]**Make Sure All Necessary Documentations Are Available:** The institution you select to apply for admission has their prerequisites for foreign students. Make sure you get to know them and prepare for it in advance. You can go to your previously attended or current most important documentation to have. Cross check your grades if it meets the minimum requirement of the institution you are aspiring for.

57 "How to prepare to study abroad" Anna Mazurek
58 "How to Prepare for Studying Abroad " internationalstudent.com

During The Application

Since you are prepared to start the journey of being a foreign student, the next step is to make a move towards achieving your aims. The following are the expected steps to be taken (Fig 8):

- **Proceed to Apply**: The first course of action to start the admission process is to set up an application at the school of your choice. Online registration is the most common means of registration by most international institutions nowadays. It would be a lot easier if you have someone in the foreign country that knows about the institution and gives you advice and also helps in the processing of the admission.

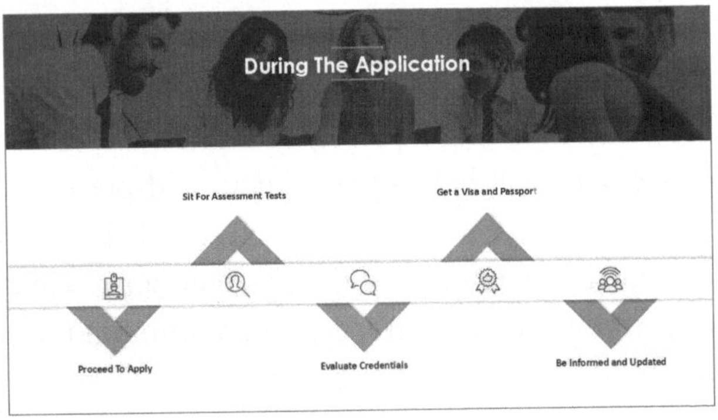

Figure 8 Roles of an Applicant: During the Application.

- **Sit For The Necessary Assessment Tests:** Once you know the demands of the institution, there is likely to be some demands that require you to sit for one or two exams like Test of English as a Foreign Language (TOEFL) or International English Language Testing System (IELTS). Almost all foreign institution programs will want you to attest that you are capable of having English Language as coursework. And perhaps you are registering for a postgraduate program, which means you are likely to sit for Graduate Record Examination (GRE) or the Graduate Management Admission Test (GMAT). Business schools require these two before you can continue your application processing.

- **Evaluate Your Credentials:** Submit your credentials to a credential evaluation agency for proper assessments of your transcripts, grades, etc. As discussed in the earlier chapter of this book, World Education Services (WES) is strongly recommended for your credential evaluation and grade conversion.
- **Get A Visa And A Passport:** It is best to start preparation at least four to five months prior to the application so as to avoid the rush of the last minute. Visa and Passport can't be acquired in a day, no matter the country you are hailing from. It takes time because there are so many paperwork and assessments you still have to go through. So, unless you have them already, make that the least of your worries by applying and getting them before beforehand.
- **Be Informed And Updated:** Information is a key factor since you are dealing with an institution that is beyond your country's borders. Submit your application at least a month in advance and make copies of all documentation. Then verify if everything needed to be done for the application has been done, then wait for a response or instructions from the institution.

After The Application

After a successful application and a successful admission offer by the University, the next step is to migrate to the country, settle for a living and get into school. However, as an international student in the institution, certain things are expected of you during your first session of being a student. They are as follows (Fig 9):

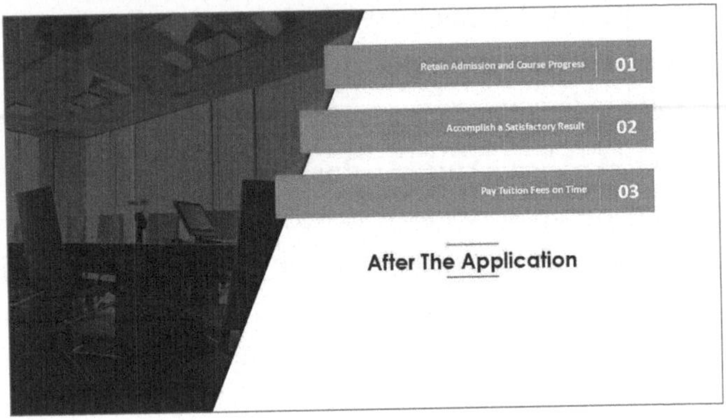

Figure 9 Roles of an Applicant: After the Application.

[59]**Retain Admission And Course Progress:** An international student must sign up for a full-time registered course at the institution. This means at least four subjects must be studied per session. Additionally, the course is expected to be completed by the specified end date given by the faculty. You may probably need to liaise with your course coordinator or the international liaison officer so as to help reduce study load. To make sure you complete your program within the time limit specified for your visa, aim for a reduced workload so you can take up more subjects in sessions to come. Moreover, if you observe it might not be possible for

59 "International student responsibilities" futurestudents.csu.edu.au

you to complete a course before the expiry date specified, meet the international student liaison officer for the appropriate guide and strategy that may help. Failure to stand by these prerequisites might lead to an inability to extend your student visa, therefore leading to the forfeiting of the program. Foreign students must complete a course at most twice the standard time stated to complete that course.

- **Accomplish A Satisfactory Result:** All foreign students are subjected to rules and policies of government acceptable academic improvement. If you are disqualified from your course, as an international student, by reason of unsatisfactory academic development, the institution will notify the appropriate quarters, and they may invalidate your student visa. International students are expected to pass the minimum of one subject in a course by the close of the second calendar year of registration for that course. International students are also expected to meet the demanded professional standards in the required fieldwork or qualified experience relating to the course. International students must excel in every core subjects in their course in no more than two trials.
- **Pay Tuition Fees On Time:** It is expected and absolutely necessary for an international student to have enough money to support and pay for his/her studies in the country. If early payment of tuition fees is not made, then admission may be annulled by the institution and appropriate departments will be notified. This might also lead to the invalidation of the student visa of the student. Those who are having an issue paying their tuition fees are expected to contact their International Student Liaison Officer for guidance.

Legalization of Credentials

[60]The legalization or certification of international degrees and studies can be defined as an act that is carried out by an experienced authority in one nation to officially acknowledge the value of a credential that is from another nation. This can involve partial or complete authentication of foreign institutions, degrees, and related certifications. There are so many official terms and agreements that uphold this act.

[61]Internationalization of the world economy has a lot to do with the movement of multitudes of people around the world nowadays. This is one of the reasons why all academic credential such as grades, diplomas, transcripts, certificates, or all other kinds of school records have to be legalized before it can be used anywhere in the world for purposes like study, work or immigration.

[62]Sometimes, the precise credential requirements may be confusing because of many complexities. An instance is when an individual was born in a particular nation, and he/she was educated in another nation, then the person immigrates to another nation looking for a job. The individual may have forfeited his indigenous citizenship or obtained new citizenship in another nation.

The following are other complexities or difficulties that may arise when it comes to the legalization of foreign credentials:

- **Transcript Unavailability**: Some institutions may not be willing to give out copies of transcripts or other

60 "Convention on the Recognition of Qualifications concerning Higher Education in the European Region" UNESCO

61 "Detecting fake university degrees in a digital world" Linda J Børresen and Stig Arne Skjerven

62 "Legalization of Educational Credentials for International Use" apostille-legalization.com

documentation for authentication more than once. They claim that they do not issue transcripts, diplomas or other school records being given at the time of completion or graduation.

- **Academic Recognition of A Program Or An Institution:** Some nations do not accept degrees from online institutions or some particular programs or institutions.
- **Corruption**: The high level of corruption in some nations has produced fake professionals. Some people possess a plausible degree without completing the program or never even attended an institution.
- **Diverse Qualification Formats:** Diversity in credential formats of degrees and transcripts from different nations sometimes deny credentials from getting legalized and recognized as a solitary document by international missions, embassies or consulates.

By reason of this, some missions, embassies, or consulates refuse to certify or validate educational qualifications straightaway. Even when the individual possesses the original copies of the credentials, it must first be validated in the nation where it was obtained by the Ministry of Education, foreign affairs, or the institution itself. Although, some countries have bodies or organizations devoted to the authentication of credentials as a necessary procedure for certification or legalization by the missions, embassies or consulates within the country.

Degree Legalization Procedure

1. Get official copies of the qualifications that have the seal of the institution on it. Make a demand for it for the purpose of international usage. Make sure they get endorsed by the institution.

2. The credentials must have the stamp of the Ministry of Education on them.
3. The foreign embassy in the country must also certify the credentials.

Identification of Fake Credentials

The use of fake degrees is not a new event. Inasmuch as competition for admission into higher education and jobs exists, a lot of people will always be desperate to take shortcuts.

What are Fake Credentials?

There are three major classifications of fake credentials. They are:

1. Credentials that appear to be issued by an institution that is accredited, however, the credentials are illegally generated. The individual who purchased the credentials has no record of studying at that particular institution.
2. Credentials that are issued by an institution that is accredited, however, the information in the documents have been altered by the credential holder, especially the grades.
3. Fake credentials issued by fake institutions (degree fraudsters). Fake institutions award 'degrees' to individuals who are willing to purchase the package; however, they have no record of academic training.

What is a Certified Educational Credential?

[63]A certified credential is the one that is gotten directly from the institution that issued it. The credential should contain an appropriate signature, date, and the institution's seal. Any credential submitted that does not satisfy these prerequisites must be labeled unofficial and be rejected and seized.

---

63 "Detecting Fraudulent Academic Credentials" Susan Byram

How do You Recognize Fake Institutions?

The reality of an institution is the principal thing that is considered during credential evaluation. There is no list of fake institutions anywhere, even if there is any; it can't be accurate. You can only recognize them by the following characteristics:

- The institution's name resembles a genuine and popular institution that exists.
- Claims are made by the institution about being recognized and accredited, or they try to disregard the importance of accreditation.
- The institution's name is made up or deceptive.
- Address of the institution frequently changes.
- The requirements for enrollment are little and not strict.
- The institution has no physical location but can be contacted only by cybernetic means.
- No tuition fee payment. Fees details are only in reference to the degree certificates.
- There is much emphasis on the institution's website about being a legit institution.
- Degrees are awarded within a short time.
- Degrees are awarded based on vocational experience alone.
- The institution pre-dates their degree documents.

Faking credentials is an act of fraud and a serious crime. The punishments for this practice are terrible. It should be avoided by all means in order not to put your career, ambition or people around you in jeopardy.

How to Deal with Fake Credentials?

Legalization of credentials is very important, that is why it is done in almost every country. It is done by either the ministry of education or the institution being applied to in that specific country. Most credential evaluators have employees that have distinctive knowledge and familiarity with different academic frameworks and are fluent in various languages which give them the ability to follow up with rational and suspicious discrepancies that appear in the academic background of an applicant.

Until a stable and robust system is built to counter fake credentials usage, fake credentials remain a threat to both the academic and business world. Nevertheless, the digital credential system initiative under development that involves securing digital credentials in a database still gives encouragement to battle fake credentials in the nearest future.

For further clarification about credential legalization, you can visit this website for more information: https://wenr.wes.org/2003/01/wenr-januaryfebruary-2003-methods-of-document-recognition-and-authentication, http://www.aic.lv/rec/Eng/leg_en/Guid_US.htm

Tuition Fees Evaluation

[64]The number of international students worldwide increases day by day, and the cost of studying in a foreign country is not becoming any lesser. Every student desires to study in an expensive country and institution, the aftereffect of that bounces on the sponsor, parents, guardian, etc. Tuition fee has an apparent variation among countries, and it would be wise for a student to carry out his/her research before speeding off to just any country, of course, unless the student has obtained financial freedom, which is quite rare.

Foreign Study Expenses in 15 Countries

Since we can't analyze the tuition fees for every country or institution in the world, this section will be discussing the top and famous 15 countries most students choose to study. Any other country not mentioned here probably has a close or similar analysis with the countries below.

Recent research reveals that the most expensive country to study is Australia. The value of education and excellence are also considered among the 15 countries in the ranking below. The ranking is also based on the average tuition fees in the top ten most significant institutions in each nation. The rating also considers the average cost of living in each town where the finest institutions are situated. Therefore, perhaps the United States higher education tuitions fee ranks the highest, the high cost of living in Australia will make it rank higher than the US in terms of countries that are expensive to study in.

---

64 "What are the most expensive study abroad destinations?" April-international

Table 5.1 shows the details of the expenses of study for an international student across countries:

Table 5.1 Total Expenses for an International Student Across Countries.

Rank	Country	Annual Higher institution costs (USD)	Annual Cost of living (USD)	Annual Total cost (USD)
1	Australia	24,081	18,012	42,093
2	Singapore	18,937	20,292	39,229
3	United States	24,914	11,651	36,564
4	United Kingdom	21,365	13,680	35,045
5	Hong Kong	13,444	18,696	32,140
6	Canada	16,746	13,201	29,947
7	France	247	16,530	16,777
8	Malaysia	2,453	10,488	12,941
9	Indonesia	4,378	8,527	12,905
10	Brazil	59	12,569	12,627
11	Taiwan	3,338	8,573	11,911
12	Turkey	1,276	10,089	11,365
13	China	3,844	6,886	10,729
14	Mexico	750	8,710	9,460
15	India	581	5,062	5,624

Some people wonder if studying in an expensive institution guarantees the best quality of education. The latest research on countries' quality rating of institution reveals that the more a country is known for its academic system, the higher the tendency that their cost of studying will increment. The fact that the most rated countries in the world are in the top five of the most expensive nations for international students to study in the world proves it. The following list contains the top ten most expensive tuition fees in the world for international students.

1. The United States of America (USA)
2. The United Kingdom
3. Australia
4. Canada
5. China
6. Singapore and France
7. Hong Kong
8. India
9. Malaysia
10. Taiwan
11. Turkey, Mexico, Indonesia, and Brazil

Credential Evaluation Organizations

There are two different globally recognized associations of credential evaluation evaluators; they are:

1. National Association of Credential Evaluation Services (NACES)
2. Association of International Credential Evaluators (AICE)

The National Association of Credential Evaluation Services (NACES) is a public organization based in the United States which endorses private firms that render, in exchange, credential evaluation services of educational degrees that are awarded in a foreign academic institution in a country outside the United States.

[65]In the US, the Department of Education is not in charge of the evaluation of international educational documentation for correspondence to qualifications awarded in the United States. Each institution in the country is charged with this responsibility. Certain institutions carry out the evaluations by themselves, and some redirect their candidates to private firms approved by NACES.

[66]The following are members of the National Association of Credential Evaluation Services (NACES). They are a group of international academic credential evaluation agencies that are devoted to quality and perfection. They are also dedicated to maintaining the standard of their vocation. They are:

1. World Education Services, Inc. (wes.org)
2. Transcript Research (transcriptresearch.com)
3. SpanTran: The Evaluation Company (spantran.com)

---

65 "Recognition of Foreign Qualifications: Information for Individuals Seeking to Study in the United States" U.S. Department of Education

66 "Directory of NACES Members" NACES

4. Josef Silny & Associates, Inc. (jsilny.com)
5. International Evaluation Service, Center for Applied Research, Evaluations, & Education, Inc. (iescaree.com)
6. International Education Research Foundation, Inc. (foreigntranscripts.com)
7. International Education Evaluations, Inc. (ierf.org)
8. International Consultants of Delaware, Inc. (icdeval.com)
9. International Academic Credential Evaluators, Inc. (iacei.net)
10. Global Services Associates, Inc. (globaleval.org)
11. Global Credential Evaluators, Inc. (gceus.com)
12. Foundation for International Services, Inc. (fis-web.com)
13. Foreign Academic Credential Service, Inc. (facsusa.com)
14. Evaluation Service, Inc. (evaluationservice.net)
15. Educational Records Evaluation Service, Inc. (eres.com)
16. Educational Perspectives, NFP (edperspective.org)
17. Educational Credential Evaluators, Inc. (ece.org)
18. Academic Evaluation Services, Inc. (aes-edu.org)
19. A2Z Evaluations, LLC (a2zeval.com)

Out of these 19 members that operate under NACES, there are three most popularly and internationally recognized credential evaluation agencies. They are:

1. [67]**World Education Services (WES):** World Education Services (WES) is a public organization that renders credential assessments services for immigrants and foreign students desiring to work or study in Canada and the United States. They have their base in Canada, New York, Toronto, and the United States.

67 "World Education Services, International Academic Credential Evaluation, Canadian Office" Peel.cioc.ca

They are the leading credential evaluation agency in North America with the record of 200,000 credentials evaluation every year. Their report permits academic institutions, employers and professional licensing boards to be fully assured and relaxed about their international applicants that have been through the agency. In one way or another, WES carries out business with thousands of academic institutions by rendering credential evaluation services and helps in global professional recruitments.

They are a vendor of 5 products, which are:

- World Education News & Reviews (WENR)
- WES International Credential Advantage Package (ICAP)
- WES Free Degree Equivalency
- WES International Grade Point Average (IGPA) Calculator

They also offer two services, which are:

- Global Talent Bridge
- WES Research & Advisory Services

2. **Academic Evaluation Services:** [68]Academic Evaluation Services (AES) is an international agency that renders assessments of international educational credentials and language translation services. The agency has a membership right with three associations, namely; Association of International Educators (NAFSA), the European Association for International Education (EAIE) and National Association of Credential Evaluation Services (NACES).

68 "Academic Evaluation Services." Aes-edu.org."

[69]AES was founded with a concentration on foreign admissions, international credential evaluations, translations, international student advising, and institution placements. It has its base in the US, and its headquarter is located in Florida. Its receiving offices are in Houston, New York, and Texas. AES renders services to their customers worldwide. AES works hand in hand with all institutions in the US. Their clients are usually those in need of foreign credential assessments for educational studies, immigration, employment, licensing for professional and military purposes. Its reputation for speed and accuracy in credential evaluations is globally famous. They conduct assessments for thousands of people from all over the world yearly.

3. **Educational Credential Evaluators (ECE):** ECE is a non-profit agency that provides evaluation reports that deal with the correspondents of academic credentials issued in a foreign country to that of the United States. It is situated in Wisconsin and was founded by James S. Frey. ECE is an approved member of NACES with the focus of initiating and managing a professional quality for private qualification assessment services. ECE has a partnership with a lot of other professional organizations in the field of foreign academics. They are as follow:

    1. American Association of Collegiate Registrars & Admissions Officers (AACRAO)
    2. National Asso ciation of Graduate Admissions Professionals (NAGAP)
    3. Association of International Educators (NAFSA)
    4. International Education Association of South Africa (IEASA)

69 "Foreign Transcript Evaluation Services - Graduate School - University of South Florida" Grad.usf.edu

5. European Association for International Education (EAIE)
6. Association of Educational Assessment in Africa (AEAA)
7. Asia-Pacific Association of International Education (APAIE)
8. Caribbean Area Network for Quality Assurance in Tertiary Education (CANQATE)

Association of International Credential Evaluators (AICE)

[70]Companies that are endorsed members of this association are not as much as NACES members. However, they are internationally accredited and recognized. AICE has ten endorsed members and 11 affiliates around the world.

Endorsed Members

1. Ucredo (ucredo.com)
2. SDR Educational Consultants (sdreducational.org)
3. Scholaro (previously known as Foreign Credits, Inc.) (scholaro.com)
4. International Evaluation Services (iesedu.org)
5. InCred Evaluations (incredevals.org)
6. Globe Language Services, Inc. (globelanguage.com)
7. Foreign Credentials Service of America (foreigncredentials.org)
8. Foreign Credential Evaluations, Inc. (fceatlanta.net)
9. American Education Research Corporation (aerc-eval.com)
10. Academic Credentials Evaluation Institute, Inc. (acei-global.org)

70 "AICE's Endorsed Member evaluation services" Association of International Credential Evaluators (AICE)

Affiliates

1. University of Wisconsin-Whitewater
2. University of West Georgia
3. University of Minnesota, Duluth
4. University of Kansas
5. University of Idaho
6. University of Arkansas
7. University of Arizona
8. iTEP International LLC
9. Credential Consultants, Inc.
10. Azusa Pacific University
11. Arizona State University

To learn more about Foreign Credentials Service in America through the EDGE database of AACRAO, visit this website: https://www.foreigncredentials.org/about-fcsa/the-edge-standard-of-evaluation.

Recapitulation and Cessation

This section closes the book, and so far, it has been able to cover a lot of things about Academic credential evaluations, and almost all possible questions have been answered. Much has been discussed on what it takes to be an international student, how to go about evaluating credentials, variations in academic systems, challenges that can be expected, grading systems, legalization of credentials, and so on. This book can be trusted as a comprehensive resource for world educational credentials where you can find all information needed in a single manuscript.

Apart from the students, several other institutions and individuals will benefit from the ideal content present in the book; USA admission officers and universities, USA employers hiring foreign graduates on H1B visas, licensors, USA state/ federal agencies, and immigration attorneys. The amount of detail on the USA academic system that has been offered by the unrivaled Dr. Korrapati will also help International educational administrators.

Snapshot of Soft Skills!

- Identify your stake-holders and maintain positive relationships with them.
- First impressions are very important.
- Being on time is imperative. This means sticking to the schedule, each time. If you are late, let it be known well in advance.
- Take notes in meetings. You will be surprised what you forget.
- Know your boundaries. Talk with your supervisor about what decisions you should or should not make. Analyze/ review expectations frequently.
- Observe and learn from others, yet create your own style. Be careful to not imbibe those traits that are likely to be detrimental.
- Have fun. Make friends. Enjoy what you do.
- Learn from your seniors on how they keep a track of the numerous tasks that they have to accomplish. Having a daily "To do" list helps.
- Before leaving messages on voice mail, write down your message and speak it slowly. For e-mails, learn when to do a "reply all" vs. "reply".
- Make a visible impact in first 100 days of your new role or job.
- Understand that it is OK to do mistakes. Ensure that you don't repeat these mistakes.
- Anything that can be measured statistically can be improved. Find a way to implement measurability.
- Criticize in private and praise in public.

- Follow-up and follow-up some more. It will highlight your dedication like nothing else.
- A hand-written thank you note is far better than an e-mail.
- Differentiate yourself from your competition to provide value to your customers. And remember that both competitors and customers can be internal.
- Plan on Monday morning; then assess and take stock on Friday. Track your weekly status without fail.
- Recommend solutions to problems and challenges and identify opportunities.
- Focus on three sides of the triangle – Employees, Customers, and Understanding your company's Business.
- Awareness on priorities will change on daily/monthly basis. Plan proactively.

Raghu's Top Ten

1) Recognize that change is an inevitable aspect of life. Learn to accept changes.
2) Make friends, especially from other cultures. Take the best from cultures and understand others' worldviews. Embracing diversity is the key to being a people's manager.
3) Get to know your managers and introduce yourself.
4) Read as much as you can; and not just your textbooks – newspapers, journals, magazines, and books that pertain to your areas of interest.
5) Travel – This is the best way to know people from your country as well as those from other countries.
6) Make good use of time. Never let a chance go to enhance your education.
7) Set annual goals to improve yourself. Have a Mission Statement as well as a Vision for your life.
8) Network extensively. Develop and maintain positive relationships with your family, coworkers, and managers in your work environment.
9) Get involved in some volunteer activities. Give back to your community and remember where you came from. Be in touch with your Alma Mater. Be socially responsible.
10) Leave your footprints on all aspects of your life (Employment, Education, and Family).

Other Books by Dr. Raghu Korrapati

What is civilization if not a vast and interlinked network of human relationships? With 'The Business of Good People', Dr. Raghu sets out to teach the reader how to make these relationships healthy and mutually beneficial. Dr. Raghu discusses certain characteristics that we all understand but fail to recognise their importance like punctuality, humility, politeness, rationality, prudence, self-supervision, persistence, apologising, assertiveness, taking the initiative, and sense of humour among others.

ISBN-10: 9350832577 **ISBN-13: 978-9350832578**

Leading an organization and its people to success remains a challenge for most managers. With organizations evolving and changing constantly it becomes even more difficult. Management theories and principles often do not provide solutions to the dilemmas that a manager has to deal with in the workplace.

This book by Dr. Raghu very adeptly gives some solid answers that managers have sought to be more successful at what they do.

ISBN-10: 8128837575 **ISBN-13: 978-8128837579**

This research applied Bayesian Modeling to medication noncompliance in glaucoma patients. A model-based decision support system using a Bayesian Network was developed to determine whether a patient was complying with the medications prescribed by the physician. The model may be generalized to other business situations where a decision has to be made based on incomplete and uncertain data sets. The purpose of this research was to devise a Bayesian framework to assess the compliance with medication in glaucoma patients.

ISBN-13: 978-0595368396 **ISBN-10: 0595368395**

This book is the essence of Dr Korrapati's 30 years of business management experience with highly successful multinational companies, coupled with distilled knowledge of his close interactions with great industry leaders. The book covers - developing a solid outsourcing strategy, deciding what to outsource, negotiating a good deal, keeping the engagement on track, ensuring access to the vendors' best resources, or even terminating a deal in a way that does not harm you. It will benefit everyone, whether you are from a firm that is looking to outsource or a vendor who seeks to establish his company as first choice partner for clients, to gain the advantage you are looking for in the fiercely competitive marketplace.

ASIN: B01JFV7JQM

Validated management Practices will walk you through the 108 required knowledge and skill areas sot that you can develop to balance the 3 critical aspects of management-employees, customers and financials, well. While some of the chapters in this book are oriented towards managers working in an Information Technology industry, it will be useful for managers in any industry with practical advice and tips on how to become an effective manager. In addition, the appendices contain extract of mandatory skills for all professionals from Dr Raghu's previous books - '108 pearls of Wisdom' and 'Dr Raghu's Top Ten' - his guiding principles.

ISBN-10: 9351654834 **ISBN-13: 978-9351654834**

While Dr Raghu Korrapati's 'Passage through India - A tryst with my soul' is an amalgam of Indian experiences of this widely travelled management guru, it is simultaneously also an exposition of his philosophical and spiritual ideas. So, as readers learn numerous lessons in sound management practice presented through Dr Raghu the leader's anecdotes and observations, he/she will be delighted to connect with Dr Raghu the man. Those familiar with Dr Raghu's previous works will be enthralled with another masterpiece on the art and science of management, this time in the context of the master's sojourn as the leader of an India IT organization. 'Passage through India' will, however, will also appeal to those who wish to understand the composer behind the composition, i.e, the mind of a man who successfully runs a large corporate organization.

ISBN-10: 9350836823 **ISBN-13: 978-9350836828**

Dr Raghu Korrapati's newest book is a seminal work that is bound to be soon accepted as a significant and powerful contribution to the literature on higher education. This is his landmark effort to encapsulate in one place all that a research scholar might need during his/her research, be it on any subject or discipline. The result is a complex and nuanced picture of the nature, processes, and contexts of research scholarship in varied departmental, disciplinary and institutional cultures.

Undoubtedly, this pivotal and pioneering book will prove to be valuable to both faculty and graduate students who study higher education. Further, institutional leaders, deans, and chairpersons of tenure, and promotion committees who seek to develop vaster comprehension of scholarship will also greatly benefit from this. Dr Korrapati has mentored thousands of research students in a wide spectrum of disciplines and fields over the span of several decades. This book by him is the latest in a long line of works that have inspired and informed innumerable students and professionals across countries.

ISBN-10: 9352617614 **ISBN-13: 9789352617616**

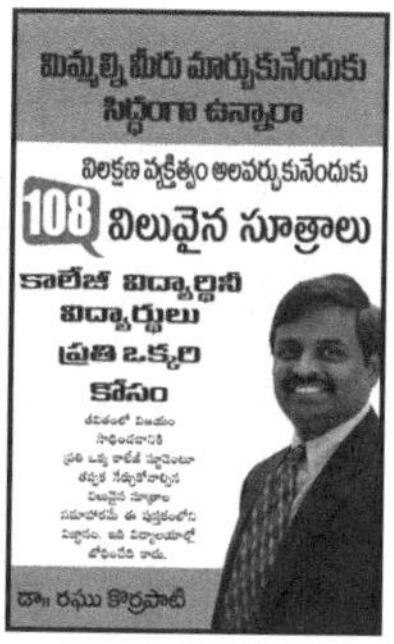

There is often a considerable gap between the aspirations that many college graduates harbor and the way they go about achieving their goals. While education and technical expertise are often ignore and that defines the difference between an average and a successful career. Dr. Raghu Korrapati has taken it upon himself to identify this 'soft' element and painstakingly elaborated upon its numerous facets. The result is this path-breaking book, which highlights the soft skills that every young graduate and professional needs to possess to reach the pinnacle of professional success. The 108 pearls of wisdom presented here have been drawn from sources as eclectic and diverse as Greek, Indian, Buddhist philosophies, modern day management theory, and psychology. This book has been translated into many languages.

ISBN-10: 8128834223 **ISBN-13: 978-8128834226**

Listed in Best Seller Category

A Master Service Agreement (MSA) is a contractual document that specifies performance objectives and outlines the responsibilities of both parties in the agreement. It also lists the current and prospective services to which the agreement applies. MSAs typically state performance objectives as service level agreements – written, measurable processes or service performance targets that the service provider and customer agree on. A statement of work (SOW) is a formal document that captures and defines the work activities, deliverables, and timeline a vendor must execute in performance of specified work for a client. The present study attempted to ascertain the factors in developing MSAs and SOWs and various best practices for alternate dispute resolutions available for offshore software managers. The study adds to the body of knowledge in the areas of Software Intellectual Property Rights, Alignment of MSAs and SOWs, ADR Mechanism for Contractual Breaches, Best Practices in Information Technology, Offshore Management, and Organizational Behavior.

ISBN-10: 1532020686 ISBN-13: 978-1532020681

The admission of foreign students to universities and colleges in the United States has two major components: the evaluation of foreign educational credentials, and the administrative process that converts the admission application into an enrolled student. The first component has historically been a source of much ambiguity and trouble for Indian students and professionals vying for places in USA Universities.

Dr Raghu Korrapati, in another glorious attempt at championing the cause of students and young professionals all over India, has come up with this seminal work to eliminate this ambiguity. In this ground-breaking book, he displays rare acumen, insight, and scholarly prowess to analyse the education systems in the USA and India, before going on to provide painstakingly researched information on each Indian higher education degree and its equivalency with respect to USA degrees. For this reason alone, this book is worth its weight in gold for any Indian student planning to study in the USA or an Indian professional aiming to work in the USA.

Apart from the students, there are numerous other institutions and individuals who will benefit from the wonderful content present in the book – USA admission officers and universities, USA employers hiring Indians on H1B visas, licensors, USA state/federal agencies, and immigration attorneys. The amount of detail on the USA education system that has been offered by the matchless Dr Korrapati will also help Indian educational administrators.

ISBN-10: 9352619870 **ISBN-13: 978-93-5261-987-0**

H-1B visas play a very important role in hiring foreign born skilled workers for Specialty Occupations in the United States. This visa system has largely benefited the U.S economy, benefitting the I.T industry the most, with the flow of skilled foreign-born employees. Due to the growing concerns over misuse and a perceived threat to domestic jobs, stricter scrutiny on H-1B petitions has increased in the past few years.

This book aims at demystifying the myths surrounding "Specialty Occupations" not only to the employers, but also to petitioners, academics, attorneys, students and other interested parties. It also aims at filling the gap in the research and understanding on Specialty Occupations. There is no comprehensive text or authority on this important issue and all the information available is only through the policy memoranda of USCIS, judgments in appealed petitioners and blogs of attorneys.

This book tries to provide a better understanding of the issue and also identifies some common errors in H-1B petitions and aims to be a one-stop reference to employers, attorneys and expert opinion evaluators on the issue

ISBN-10: 9352787706 **ISBN-13: 978-93-5278-778**

This book is updated version of previous years book. Based on receiving huge compliments from prior version, this book includes updates for years 2019-20. Several new guidelines in the area of Minimum Requirements for proffered position, Interview requirements for Specialty occupations questionnaire, sample job description templates, Guidelines on generic "Engineering" or "Business Administration" degrees, and new requirements for evaluators.

This book aims at demystifying the myths surrounding "Specialty Occupations" not only to the employers, but also to petitioners, academics, attorneys, students and other interested parties. It also aims at filling the gap in the research and understanding on Specialty Occupations. There is no comprehensive text or authority on this important issue and all the information available is only through the policy memoranda of USCIS, judgments in appealed petitioners and blogs of attorneys.

This book tries to provide a better understanding of the issue and also identifies some common errors in H-1B petitions and aims to be a one-stop reference to employers, attorneys and expert opinion evaluators on the issue.

ISBN-10: 9352969227 ISBN-13: 978-93-5296-922-7

There is tremendous ambiguity surrounding this field. It is compounded by the fact that grading systems differ widely in theory and practice from one country to another, and the fair interpretation of foreign grades into national ones is a major concern, both for students returning after a study period abroad and for university staff required to assess the credentials of foreign applicants. The academic world, especially students, struggle to determine what their education amounts to in another country.

The credential evaluation component also exists outside of the academic community: at state licensing boards and other types of governmental agencies, at professional associations, and at private foreign educational credential evaluation services which assist institutions and agencies that do not have in-house expertise. This book is also aimed to facilitate the smoother functioning of these institutions.

ISBN-10: 9352969219 ISBN-13: 978-93-5296-921-0

It is often said that salespeople would rather sell than spend a day learning how to do it. They think time is money and every hour spent in training is money lost and time wasted. But what they fail to understand is that learning how to do sales effectively is actually a catalyst for great sales results for the organization and excellent sales performance for the individual. It is worth noting that while sales is one of the easiest careers to get into, it is not as easy to sustain and spend a life in. So to put it in simpler words, ***"Everyone can be a sales person, but not everyone can be a successful sales person".*** To be a successful salesperson it is important to have a deep understanding of the industry you cater to. While the general skill set remains the same, it is the deeper and niche understanding that has the power to differentiate the best from the rest.

In the market, there are numerous books and articles on various sales techniques available. In this book, I am discussing the 'Nine habits of highly effective software sales professionals'. The title gives you a broad idea of what this book is all about, but more than nine habits, it is packed with 30 years of my personal and professional experience in the software industry and managing clients. I provided more emphasis on how successful sales professionals, sales leaders and their companies organize themselves with short-term and long-term planning and adopt disciplined execution on those plans.

ISBN-10: 9352969200 ISBN-13: 978-93-5296-920-3

Notes